BEERS
OF THE WORLD

BEERS
OF THE WORLD

GILBERT DELOS

Photography
Matthieu Prier

TIGER BOOKS INTERNATIONAL
LONDON

Translated from the French by Simon Knight,
in association with First Edition Translations Ltd, Cambridge

3455
This edition published in 1994 by Tiger Books International PLC, London
Produced by Copyright SARL, Paris
© 1994 English language edition, CLB Publishing, Godalming, Surrey
All rights reserved
ISBN 1 85501 420 3
Printed and bound in Singapore by Tien Wah Press

TABLE OF CONTENTS

THE STORY OF LIQUID BREAD

The earliest record of brewing comes to us from the ancient Sumerians, written in cuneiform characters on clay tablets over six thousand years ago. But it is quite likely that beer has an even longer history.

It was probably first brewed in Neolithic times, when early man began to harvest cereals and keep them for later consumption. By cooking the grain and letting it ferment in water, our primitive ancestors produced a nutritious and thirst-quenching beverage that did not deteriorate easily. A drink so closely bound up with the cultivation of cereals was not surprisingly referred to as 'liquid bread'. *Sikaru*, the beverage consumed by the Sumerians in their settlements between the Tigris and the Euphrates (in present-day Iraq), was already a sophisticated product. Almost twenty varieties are recorded, with such specific uses as feeding the sick, paying temple construction-site workers and honouring the gods. The British Museum possesses two stone carvings at least five thousand years old (the Blau monument), which show beer being offered to the goddess Nin-Harra.

Above: mural painting from the tomb of Sennedjem, Egypt: Sennedjem and his wife reaping. *Valley of the Kings, Thebes.*
Left: Egyptian woman preparing beer, c. 2500 BC. *Archaeological Museum, Florence.*

The Babylonian Empire, which superseded the Sumerian, has left us some fascinating insights into the social importance of beer, particularly in the legal code of King Hammurabi, founder of the first Babylonian dynasty (c. 1730 BC). One article prescribes exemplary punishments for brewers guilty of malpractice: they might be drowned in their own beer if it were judged unfit to drink. And the death penalty was also applicable to a priestess caught in a beer shop! In Babylonian society, a brewer was a man of some standing, even exempt from military service, on condition that he supply campaigning armies with 'loaves [or cakes] of beer'. This term is explained by the way beer was made in ancient times, a technique described in minute detail by the Egyptians in fresco paintings and papyrus documents.

The malted cereals (barley, millet or spel – a variety of wheat) were coarsely ground into flour, then shaped into loaves [cakes] and cooked in the oven, so that they could be kept and transported. To transform them into beer, the loaves [cakes] were broken up, steeped in water, and allowed to ferment for several days. The drink obtained in this way can have had little in common with the clear, carbonated beers we know today. It was dark and cloudy, with solid residues held in

FROM SIKARU TO BEER

The ancient Sumerian term for cereal-based fermented beverages seems to have had no derivatives, apart perhaps from the Hebrew word *shekar*, meaning 'to get drunk'. Similarly, the Egyptian terms *zythu* and *courmi*, the camon or millet-beer drunk by Attila the Hun, the *xytho* of the Scythians and the rye-based *kwasz* of the Slavs have all disappeared without trace. For a time, the *cerveza* of the Iberians almost became the generally adopted term due to the universality of Latin, from which is derived the *cervoise* dear to the Gauls.

There is some controversy over the origin of the word 'beer'. Of Germanic origin, it may have come from the Old Teutonic *bewo*, the Old Saxon *bere*, or the Netherlandish *beura* or *beuza*. All these terms are in any case related to the word for barley, the prime cereal used in beer making, as is the Old English term *beor*, which coexisted with the Gallic *cervoise*.

suspension. From the time of the first dynasty (3300 BC), beer was an indispensable element in Egyptian ceremonies honouring the dead; Isis was worshipped as protectress of cereals, and Osiris as patron deity of brewers. 'In my dignity as Master of all, I receive offerings from my altars, I drink jugs of beer at dusk': thus speaks the god Atoum in the *Book of the dead*. In the *Book of dreams*, thoughts of beer during the hours of sleep are

considered to be a favourable omen.

The Egyptians made various kinds of beer, under the general name of *zythum*. The clearest type was the drink of the poor, while varieties spiced with ginger, dates or honey were reserved for persons of high rank. As the Ebers papyrus proves, beer was an essential item in the treatment of the sick, particularly those suffering from skin and eye ailments. At a later date, the ancient city of Pelusium (near present-day Port Said) was an important brewing centre, exporting its beers throughout the Mediterranean.

Almost half way round the world, the Chinese were also producing beer during this period (almost four thousand years ago), and using techniques far in advance of their Mediterranean counterparts. Early texts mention a clear, fully-fermented beverage based on millet: *tsiou*, more an intoxicating liquor than liquid daily bread. It was supposed to be reserved for offerings to the ancestors, and the death penalty could be imposed on those who abused it.

A WOMAN'S PLACE ...

Since time immemorial, the brewing of beer was the preserve of women, and fittingly so for a drink so nourishing and nutritious. While the menfolk hunted and made war, the women stayed at home and prepared the various foodstuffs, not least beer. Though drunk in large quantities at male gatherings, beer could be brewed only by women. Nor was the woman's function merely that of domestic drudge. According to the Belgian historian Marcel Gocar, 'there was a time when beer was drunk in temples, served by priestesses'. The ritual function is also found among the Incas of South America, where only virgins devoted to the Sun were allowed to prepare the corn beer drunk by the emperor. Earlier still, in ancient Babylon, beer houses evolved as the first bars, and the first brothels: their inmates, the *tsabitu*, brewed the precious liquid, as well as offering sexual services to their customers. In ancient times, when religion and mysticism permeated daily life, women's role in preparing beer had a powerful ritual dimension. This was symbolised by the cauldron, which, according to the ethnologist Claude Lévi-Strauss, represents the 'universal whole'. Because woman's function as giver of life was regarded as no less than magical, she was also seen as having the power to transform cereals, in the depths of her household cauldron, into an intoxicating, thirst-quenching drink. We encounter a striking instance of this myth in the Scandinavian legend of Valhalla: heroes slain in combat rise to immortality as a result of drinking beer from the cauldron of the Valkyries. But as Christianity took hold in Europe and, with it, wine, women's special status in the brewing of beer gradually diminished. Emblematic of this change is the story of Katherina von Bora: when she married the reformer Martin Luther, she had to give up the occupation of brewer she had previously exercised in a monastery. The old customs died hard: until the 16th century in Northern Germany, brewing utensils were part of a young woman's dowry; and as late as the 19th century in the province of Mecklembourg, a young wife would recite this prayer on first entering her new home: 'Our Lord / When I brew, help the beer / When I knead, help the bread'.

In Britain, the tradition of women brewers, or ale wives, also lingers in the collective memory, and some are known by name: Maggy, a Scottish lass

For many years, advertisers have urged women to drink beer on the grounds that it aids lactation.

who, in the 16th century, asked the poet Buchanan to help her recover her lost clientele; Alice Causton, pilloried for having cheated on the standard measure; or Elizabeth, mother of Oliver Cromwell, Lord Protector of the ephemeral English Commonwealth.

Whereas in traditional societies women continue to brew fermented beverages – using maize in Mexico and South America, cassava in Amazonia, sorghum or green bananas in Africa – sooner or later more advanced civilisations deprive them of this role and entrust it exclusively to men.

OF WARRIORS AND MONKS

For reasons still largely unexplained, the Greek and Roman civilisations were the first to turn their backs on beer and accord preference to wine. Pliny the Elder contemptuously dismisses beer as 'barley wine'! Wine, symbol of the blood of Christ, spread across Europe in the wake of Christianity, while beer became the drink of the vanquished, of benighted barbarians lost in the northern mists. During the first millenium AD, the Scandinavians, Celts and Germans were the last bastion of brewing culture in Europe. Among them, beer

their skulls. When setting out on an expedition in their *drakkars*, the Danish and Norwegian Vikings always took a number of barrels, to enable them to brew beer as the need dictated. And it is to the Celts that we owe technical progress in malting, the vital operation whereby the grain germinates, transforming starch into fermentable sugars. (The Celtic word for malt, *braces*, is in fact the origin of the French words for brewing and brewery: 'brassage' and 'brasserie').

Although the Christian religion robbed beer of its sacred connotations, transferring them to wine, it nevertheless retained the use of beer as a thirst-quenching drink. The monastic communities that spread throughout Europe in the fifth century began brewing beer for their own needs and eventually produced the drink on a large scale. At a time when water supplies were often suspect, the brewing process guaranteed a wholesome – and far more agreeable – drink. The Greek and Latin manuscripts in monastery libraries contained records of Egyptian practices, enabling the monks to perfect their own techniques. This is attested to by a remarkable document: a plan of the abbey of Sankt Gallen, in Switzerland, dating from the ninth century, which clearly shows the existence of a malting and three brew houses. Each contains a

remained sacred, a reward for heroes and an offering worthy of the gods. Drinking horns, some holding over two litres, continued to be passed from hand to hand at interminable banquets, as warriors recounted their heroic exploits. Beer is at the heart of many a brutal and violent saga: in the Scandinavian Sigurd cycle, Gudrun takes vengeance of Atli by making him drink the blood of his children, mixed with beer and served in

large mash tun, a cooling tank and a fermentation vessel. Here, the monks prepared three different beers: the best, or *prima melior*, brewed from barley, was reserved for distinguished guests; the second, *cervisia*, was made from oats and satisfied the daily needs of the monks; the third, known as *tertia*, was served to pilgrims.

The obligation to offer board and lodging to all comers was a factor in deciding monasteries to opt

THE MORE SAINTS THE MERRIER

Lacking respect for beer, the Greeks and Romans ascribed to it no specific deity, equivalent of Dionysus or Bacchus in the case of wine. But many other civilisations – the Incas, Scandinavians or Chinese – regarded beer as an indispensable element in their intercessions with the gods. In Europe, the first lay brewers were anxious to win the favour of the Christian religion, which gave a privileged position to wine, by choosing appropriate patron saints for their trade: in Ireland, St Columba, who is said to have introduced beer to many European monasteries in the 6th century; in Austria and Bavaria, St Florian; in Munich, St Boniface; in Northern Germany, St Lawrence or St Vith; in Alsace, St Leonard, and so on.
There are even two St Arnoulds associated with beer: one from Lorraine, born in Metz in 580, who miraculously filled the jugs and goatskins of the faithful who followed his funeral procession; the other from Tiegem, born in 1040, who is venerated in Flanders and Wallonia for changing polluted water into beer in order to heal the sick.

for beer, less costly and more readily available than wine. With the development of the major pilgrimage routes, travellers' preference for a particular convent or monastery contributed greatly to its fame, and the quality of the beer was a far from negligible factor in determining the pilgrims' choice. Such monasteries were the setting for two major technical innovations, marking progress from primitive brews to the kind of beer we appreciate today. The first, around the year 1000, was the introduction of hops, which were gradually to replace all the other herbs and spices previously used to flavour beer; then, in the 15th century, the technique of bottom fermentation was developed in a Bavarian convent not far from Munich.

Several church councils promulgated regulations restricting the consumption of beer in monasteries,

for instance the Council of Aix-la-Chapelle in 817, but since they were renewed century by century we may safely assume that such injunctions were largely ignored.

THE TRADE OF BREWER

Breweries began to be established in European towns between the 11th and 13th centuries. Although home brewing continued in the countryside, the growth of urban centres led to specialisation, with sufficient customers concentrated in one area to make brewing a rewarding occupation.

The first officially recorded brewer, according to a document of 1259, is Arnoldus of Strasbourg. By 1267, Strasbourg boasted a 'Beer Street', with stone-built houses – unusual for the period – on account of the fires needed to heat the vats. Brewers, known as 'cambiers', appear in the municipal regulations of Amiens in the early 12th century, while in Paris statutes governing their activities were first published in 1268. In Germany, Frankfurt is recorded as having a brewery in 1288 and, less than a century later, Munich had no less than three. Under pressure from the feudal lords, the Church and monasteries were gradually forced to renounce their privileges as brewers and were no longer permitted to serve beer free of charge. In 974, the emperor Otto II granted brewing rights to the town of Liège. Brewing was already a highly profitable activity, and a useful source of taxation revenue. The early lay brewers were therefore quick to complain of the monks, who paid for neither grain nor labour.

In London, and at Trondheim in Norway, brewers' guilds were first founded in the 11th century.

Detail of a basket of hops. Musée des Beaux-Arts, Lille.

18th-century Belgian bronze statue symbolising beer. The woman is holding some hop flowers in her left hand. Musée des Beaux-Arts, Lille.

These mutual aid associations soon developed into powerful corporations, which flourished throughout the medieval period. The Bruges guild was established in 1308, and its Liège counterpart in 1357. The right to brew beer was not easily won. For one thing, regulations were introduced: in Strasbourg, pursuant to a municipal edict that remained in force until the Revolution, brewing was only permitted between St Michael's day (29 September) and the feast of St George (23 April). This was because hot weather upsets the fermentation process in the absence of effective refrigeration.

Brewers also regulated their profession by introducing an apprenticeship system. In Paris in 1514, for instance, three years was stipulated as the time needed to learn the trade. This system was seriously threatened by Louis XIV: anxious to raise revenue, the king decided that a brewing monopoly should be sold to the highest bidder. The traditional training was in danger of being replaced by an authorisation permitting anybody to brew beer – irrespective of qualification – provided he could pay for the privilege. The danger passed, however, and the general trend of legislation has always been to safeguard the quality of beer. In Artois in 1550, a regulation was published forbidding brewers to use lime or soap. Then, in 1516, William, prince elector of Bavaria, promulgated his famous purity law – the *Rheinheitsgebot* – obliging brewers to use no ingredients other than barley, water and hops. This edict is still in force, and right down to the present day has been a factor in protecting German brewers from foreign competition.

The towns also instituted quality control regulations, with inspectors authorised to make lightning visits to test the wholesomeness of the product. *Ale-tasters* in Britain, *eswarts* in Flanders and *bierkieser* in Alsace sometimes employed such original methods as pouring a few drops of beer onto their chair then sitting on it. If, after an hour, their trousers were well and truly stuck, the beer was reckoned to be of high enough density; if not, it had to be poured away, or sold at a lower price.

While the professional brewers sold their wares mainly from a tavern adjacent to the brewery, they had to compete with other unauthorised traders, who retailed beer produced by womenfolk in the home.

The beers of this period were drunk new and in

Left: Drinkers, *by the Flemish painter Jan Baptist Lambrechts (1680 – post 1731). Musée Crozatier, Le Puy-en-Vallée.*

Below: Still life with a glass of beer *(1644), by the Dutch painter Pieter Claesz. Musée des Beaux-Arts, Nantes.*

the immediate vicinity of the brew house, since they travelled badly. This explains the proliferation of small-scale breweries in the towns, and the suppression of corporations at the time of the French Revolution encouraged a further increase in their numbers.

GAMBRINUS, KING OF BREWERS

Lacking a tutelary deity, beer nevertheless has its king in the person of Gambrinus, a mythical figure who sits astride a beer barrel, beer mug in hand. He made his first appearance in Nuremberg in 1543, in a celebrated poem by Burkart Waldis.

Though there is no serious evidence for Gambrinus as a historical figure, he is generally identified with Duke John I of Brabant who, in the 13th century, celebrated a military victory with a great banquet, at which beer flowed in rivers.

Though familiar throughout Europe at the close of the Middle Ages, Gambrinus was not fully exploited for his publicity value until the 19th century, when brewers began using this epitome of conviviality and bonhomie to affirm the quality of their beers.

A REVOLUTION IN TECHNOLOGY

The brewing techniques in use at the beginning of the 19th century had changed little since the Middle Ages. Brewers were producing small quantities of top-fermentation beers, mostly of amber or brown coloration, mainly in the winter season, and generally for local consumption. The next few decades were to see radical changes: in the nature and style of beers, in production methods, in distribution, and in the economics of the profession generally. Scientific discoveries and technological progress followed thick and fast. Central Europe was the powerhouse of this revolution, with Czechoslovakia, Germany and Austria setting the pace and creating a new kind of beer that was quickly to take the world by storm. Whereas so-called top-fermentation beers were brewed at between 15 and 20°C, in 1842 brewers in the Czech town of Pilsen invented a bottom-fermentation process, brewing at between 7 and 12°C to produce a beer distinguished by its attractive golden coloration and limpidity. The Austrian brewer Anton Dreher perfected a similar technique at around the same time. Bottom-fermentation had been known since the 15th century, but it required a considerable cooling capacity, whether by natural or artificial means. Progress in transport during the 19th century enabled brewers to import snow and ice from the mountains and store it in underground cold rooms. In Strasbourg in 1867, for instance, there were as many as 46 cold stores of this kind, with a total capacity of 100,000 hectolitres. It is calculated that in 1875 American breweries consumed 30 million tons of ice!

A steam engine of the kind invented by Scotsman James Watt was in use as early as 1830 in Gabriel Sedlmayr's Spaten brewery in Munich, making it possible to increase production by achieving more constant temperatures. In 1873, his son was the first to install a refrigeration plant, freeing him from dependence on supplies of natural ice. The development of railways also revolutionised the brewing industry in the second half of the century. Beer could now be transported rapidly to slake the thirst of the big industrial towns: in 1869,

Le Bock, by Picasso (1901). Pushkin Museum, Moscow.

THE BREWERS' STAR

Many breweries in Northern France, Germany and, especially, Alsace are distinguished by a six-pointed star formed from two superimposed triangles. This star, which first appeared on brewers' premises in the 15th century, can have no connection with the Star of David, symbol of modern Judaism, if only because, from early times, Jews were forbidden to brew and sell beer.

The brewers' star is far more likely to derive from an alchemist's symbol, Solomon's Seal, which breaks down into the four basic elements – fire, water, earth and air – involved in the different stages of brewing. The star is therefore a kind of talisman, reassuring the brewer that his beer will be prepared according to the rules of the art.

The word star itself is also often associated with beer, for instance Stella Artois in Belgium, Lone Star in the United States and, simply, Star in Nigeria.

barely ten years after the inauguration of the Strasbourg-Paris line, the Alsace breweries were sending almost 300,000 hectolitres a year to the French capital, where their lager beers were all the rage.

Science then came to the aid of the brewers. Their product was frequently spoilt during fermentation, and no one could account for such accidents. At the request of brewers in Northern France, Louis Pasteur set his mind to solving this problem. As well as discovering the role of yeasts in fermentation, he demonstrated the need to protect beer from infectious contaminations. He therefore advised rigorous standards of hygiene in breweries and introduced the pasteurisation process, which keeps beer from deteriorating for several months after production. Following in his footsteps, around 1880 the Dane Emile Hansen, who worked in the Carlsberg breweries, isolated the different strains of yeast, enabling brewers to produce beer more intelligently and renew this essential raw material at regular intervals.

In Germany, Belgium and Great Britain the two styles of beer have co-existed quite happily down to the present day. This has not been the case in the rest of Europe or in North America, where bottom-fermentation blond beers, known as pilsners or lagers, quickly won general acceptance. Refreshing and with a distinct head, lager beer proved more attractive than other types, and in the 20th century has become the world's standard of reference. Almost everywhere – America, Africa and Asia included – it has usurped the place of more traditional brews.

The growth in consumption called for enormous industrial resources. Brewers with the necessary clout soon forced out their inefficient or backward-looking rivals. France is an extreme case: in 1905, there were still 3,543 brewers; today only a score remain. Moreover, the three biggest account for almost 90 percent of total production, in vast factories equipped with the latest technology. Standardisation of production has led to a worldwide loss of variety: in Tokyo and Los Angeles, Paris and Cape Town, there is a tendency for all beers to taste alike, competing more with soft drinks than with other authentic products of a grand tradition stretching back thousands of years.

Be that as it may, the vast monolith of lager brewing has not completely supplanted the rich

heritage of traditional beers still to be found in all parts of the world. Since the 1970s, a movement to rediscover them has grown and developed, to the point where Michael Jackson – a world specialist who has doubtless tasted more beers than any other man alive – can speak of a veritable renaissance. Old or traditional styles of beer are being rediscovered and increasingly exported from one country to another. Meanwhile, in the United States, Britain and Germany, a large number of non-industrial 'micro-breweries' have sprung up, selling their wares only on the premises – a welcome throwback to the Middle Ages.

Poster advertising the Brasserie Phénix, Marseille, showing how brewing became a full-scale industry at the end of the last century.

TAKE WATER, MALT
AND HOPS …

In essentials, the brewing of beer has not changed since the Middle Ages, nor even since the time of the Sumerians. The trick is still to transform cereals into a thirst-quenching, flavoursome and more or less alcoholic beverage by harnessing the process of fermentation. Differences in taste, flavour and colour are all due to techniques and practices associated with individual countries, styles of beer and master brewers. Regardless of climate, season and even place of origin, brewing is entirely a question of know-how, whether handed down over generations or based on the latest technology.

Expression par excellence of human ingenuity, brewing also has symbolic connotations, which some authors trace back to the ancient practice of alchemy. What is beyond dispute is that, while a wine is the expression of its native soil, each beer has its origins in a specific cultural setting.

Heineken's grand brewing hall at Schiltigheim (formerly the Brasserie de l'Espérance), resplendent in copper and stained glass.

Barley, the raw material universally used in brewing beer.

The hop is a fast-growing vine, reaching a height of five to seven metres.

The cone-shaped flower clusters contain the essential oils used in flavouring beer.

HOPS: IMPARTING FLAVOUR

Though often thought of as the main ingredient in beer, hops are really an additive: 100 to 300 grammes are sufficient to flavour 100 litres, a mere hundredth of the quantity of malt required. The common hop *(Humulus lupulus)* is a quick-growing plant, reaching from five to seven metres in height. It is the cone-shaped female flowers that are mainly used in brewing, though British producers still use male hops.

Small though it may be, the hop cone contains a wealth of resins and essential oils; in fact more than two hundred aromatic components have been identified. It is these that turn the sugary juices resulting from the brewing process into flavoursome beers.

Cereals are the raw material most commonly used in brewing. Although wheat, rye, cassava, millet, sorghum, rice, maize and even green bananas are still used to produce alcoholic drinks with some resemblance to beer, the mainstay of the brewing industry worldwide is barley.

Before it can be used to brew beer, barley has to be made into malt, thereby transforming its starch content into fermentable sugars. After steeping in water, it is left to germinate in a warm environment, then heated in a process called kilning, which gives a more or less dark colour to the malt and likewise to the resulting beer.

The malt obtained in this way is milled into a fine

grist, then mixed with hot water: this is the brewing operation proper, lasting between one and two hours. It is performed in large mash tuns, some of which are still made of copper, with the characteristic chimney serving to evacuate steam. Once the solid residues (known as returns) have been filtered out, the liquid, or wort, is heated in a copper to over 100°C and hops are incorporated. On cooling, yeast is added to the liquid and it is allowed to ferment in another vessel, until the sugars have been transformed into alcohol and carbon dioxide.

After further filtering, the resulting 'green beer' is left to rest and mature, before being packaged into casks or bottles and, in some cases, pasteurised to improve its travelling qualities.

This is the basic procedure used in brewing almost all types of beer. Of course, there are many variants, and it is these that will determine the characteristics of a particular product.

The choice of barley, the type of malt (pale or dark), the addition of other cereals (maize, rice) or of maltose syrups, the variety of hop (more or less bitter or aromatic), the duration of the brewing process and the chosen temperature are all vital factors in determining the final properties of a beer.

The most important stage is undoubtedly fermentation, since it is this that dictates the type of beer that will result. There are two main types of fermentation:

top fermentation, the older of the two, is effected at 15-20°C over a relatively short period (three to five days), with yeasts that rise to the surface of the beer. It produces beers that are dense, full-flavoured and long in the mouth;

bottom fermentation, the most widely practised method nowadays, takes between seven and ten days at lower temperatures (6-8°C). The yeasts remain at the bottom of the fermentation vessel.

There is also a third – 'spontaneous' – fermentation process, employed in Belgium to produce lambic

To transform barley into malt, the grain is allowed to germinate on the vast floor areas of the malting.

The wort being boiled in a copper.

WATER SUPPLY

For many years, the quality of the local water supply was an important factor in brewing, which explains why quite small towns, such as Burton upon Trent, could be home to several breweries (including the giant Bass company). The Strasbourg region owes its position as the major centre of French brewing to the purity and extent of the local groundwater table.

Modern technology has freed brewing from this constraint, making it possible to improve and purify the local water supply as required. However, a copious supply of water is still essential: it takes at least six or seven litres of water to produce one litre of beer, both for the brewing process proper and for flushing out and cleaning the various vessels used. Since the time of Pasteur, absolute cleanliness has been the watchword in breweries throughout the world.

Brew kettle at the Kronenbourg brewery, with its characteristic chimney.

DENSITY AND ALCOHOLIC CONTENT

To measure the alcoholic strength of a beer, for many years brewers used a system for calculating its density, i.e. the relationship between the volumes of cereals and water used in the brewing process. This is logical, since it can be expected to indicate the amount of alcohol present. Such systems, with measurements given in degrees Plato or degrees Balling, are still in use in Britain and Germany. French brewers indicate the strength of their beer in degrees Régie, a method more akin to that used for measuring the alcoholic content of other types of drink: one degree represents one cubic centimetre of pure alcohol in 100 cubic centimetres of beer.

The brewers' reticence is explained by the relative instability of their product, whose alcoholic content can vary over time.

It is also possible to quantify the bitterness of a beer using the EUB (European Units of Bitterness) system: 10 EUBs would indicate a somewhat insipid beer, 40 EUBs a very bitter one.

Colour is not a reliable indicator of alcoholic strength: many pale beers are a great deal stronger than brown ales or Irish stouts.

and gueuze beers. It relies on yeasts which occur naturally in the atmosphere in a restricted region to the south of Brussels.

Finally, some brewers add yeast when the beer is bottled. This causes a secondary fermentation, evidenced by a sediment (the lees) which accumulates on the bottom of the bottle.

Pasteurisation, which requires heating the liquid to a high temperature for a very short period, has the disadvantage of sterilising the beer and, worse, of destroying its subtle aromas. There are now more modern methods of filtering and drawing off the beer in sterile conditions so that it can travel without risk of deterioration.

In the case of alcohol-free beers, one of two main techniques is employed: either the alcohol is removed from the finished beer, or fermentation is interrupted at a very early stage, resulting in a beery taste and a very low alcohol content. In either case, highly technical processing and considerable expertise are involved.

Depending on its duration and the kind of casks used, the conditioning stage is also very important in determining the nature of a beer. It lasts between two and twelve weeks for common or

garden beers but, as practised by some Belgian and British brewers, may extend to several months or even two years, the beer being kept in oak casks.

Once bottled, beer must be stored away from sources of heat and light and cannot be kept for more than a few months, except in the case of certain abbey beers from Belgium or some special British ales.

The food value of beer compared with other drinks (Musée de Stenay).

THE MAIN CLASSES OF BEERS

TOP FERMENTATION:
– Ales :
  pale, mild, bitter,
  porter, barley wine, stout
– Altbier
– Special brews :
  trappiste,
  abbey, red,
  bières de garde
– Wheat beers :
  white, Weizen, Weisse

BOTTOM FERMENTATION:
– Lager :
  pilsner, Dortmunder,
  malt liquor
– Vienna, March beer
– Munich, Bock, Dopple Bock,
  Rauchbier

SPONTANEOUS FERMENTATION: lambic, gueuze, faro, kriek

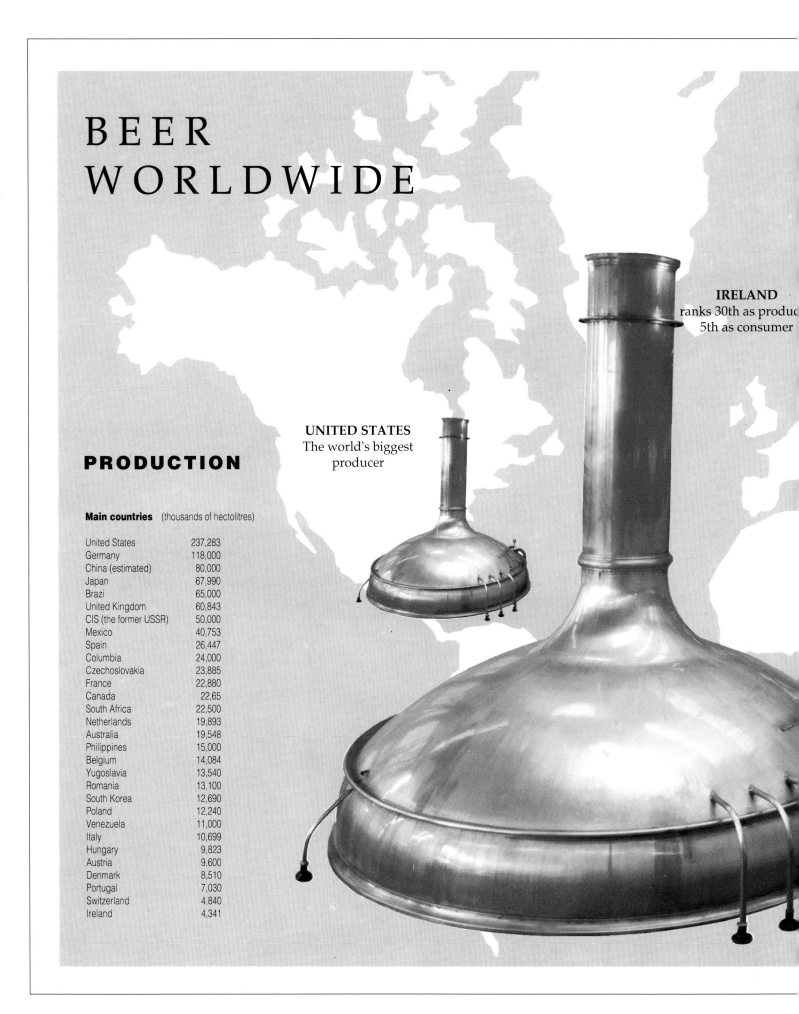

BEER
WORLDWIDE

IRELAND
ranks 30th as produc
5th as consumer

UNITED STATES
The world's biggest
producer

PRODUCTION

Main countries (thousands of hectolitres)

United States	237,283
Germany	118,000
China (estimated)	80,000
Japan	67,990
Brazi	65,000
United Kingdom	60,843
CIS (the former USSR)	50,000
Mexico	40,753
Spain	26,447
Columbia	24,000
Czechoslovakia	23,885
France	22,880
Canada	22,65
South Africa	22,500
Netherlands	19,893
Australia	19,548
Philippines	15,000
Belgium	14,084
Yugoslavia	13,540
Romania	13,100
South Korea	12,690
Poland	12,240
Venezuela	11,000
Italy	10,699
Hungary	9,823
Austria	9,600
Denmark	8,510
Portugal	7,030
Switzerland	4,840
Ireland	4,341

From the 148 litres drunk annually by the average German (and the adult Bavarian is reckoned to down 240!) to the small quantity consumed by the average Chinese, national disparities in both production and consumption are enormous. This is explained by the fact that, though beer is the most widely consumed of all beverages, each country has its own beer culture.

GERMANY
the world's biggest
consumer

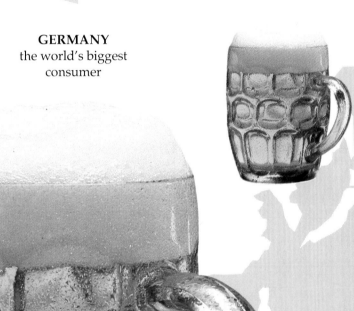

CHINA
ranks only 29th
as a consumer,
with 6.7 litres drunk
per head

CONSUMPTION

Main countries	(litres per head per annum)
Germany	148.6
Czechoslovakia	132.3
Netherlands	132
Denmark	127.2
Ireland	123.9
Austria	122.7
Belgium	120
Australia	112.7
United Kingdom	110
Hungary	95
United States	93.9
Canada	83.6
Spain	72.8
Columbia	71.4
Portugal	65.2
South Africa	62.3
Yugoslavia	57.6
Romania	56.5
Japan	54.8
Venezuela	54.3
Mexico	46.4
Brazil	42.3
France	40.1
CIS (the former USSR)	33.7
Poland	31.4
South Korea	29.3
Philippines	23.8
Italy	18.7
China (estimated)	6.7

EUROPE

Although there is no disputing the role of Mesopotamia and Egypt in pioneering the art of brewing several thousand years ago, it is undoubtedly Europe that has produced the greatest diversity of fine beers – and the greatest beer drinkers. In the northern parts of the continent – from London to Munich, via Flanders, Alsace and Czechoslovakia – the connoisseur can sample an enormous range of styles, brewed in many different ways. Here, the art has been brought to an unparalleled degree of refinement. While the types of beer invented in Europe – whether Czechoslovakian pilsners, Munich ambers or Irish stouts – have been imitated all round the world, the biggest brewing concerns, such as Heineken and Carlsberg, all claim Europe as their native soil.

In Strasbourg, the Eurobeer Show, held every other year in April, has become a meeting place for members of the brewing profession from throughout the continent, encouraging respect for the traditions of each country and increased international trade. This is no time for insularity and introversion, but for discovery and dissemination of the industry's finest products. There is much still to be done before German Weissbier, British ale, Brussels gueuze and Flemish *bière de garde* are as widely known and appreciated as they deserve.

GREAT BRITAIN

Britain's geographical separation from the rest of Europe finds an echo in her approach to beer. While other nations have succumbed to the temptations of low-fermentation lagers, the British have remained faithful to their ancient top-fermentation beers, or ales, which are still produced in a number of distinct styles. In fact, when the big brewers wanted to modernise their products, the opposition of beer drinkers was strong, organised and ultimately crowned with success.

This can be understood only if one appreciates the importance of the pub, high place of beer drinking and of British social life generally. Money may have gone decimal, the Channel Tunnel may be with us, but it will be many a year before the ritual of the pub changes one iota. Many traditional ales sold in pubs are available only on draught and cannot be found in bottled form, which is in itself a guarantee of stability.

Continental lagers are making inroads in Britain, however, and seem to have found favour with the younger generation: cans and cans of the stuff are consumed before, during and after football matches.

Although industrial takeovers have led, as everywhere, to the disappearance of many independent breweries, this has not diminished the number of different styles of beer, which in Britain vary from region to region. Here as nowhere else, the way for a beer drinker to familiarise himself with the magnificent traditions of the national brewing industry is to go on a pub crawl and sample the local wares.

At the bar, by British artist John-Henry Henshall (1856-1928). Christopher Wood Gallery, London.

ALES

On first encounter, a British ale takes the continental visitor by surprise: this beer has very little head, is low in alcohol, slightly cloudy, and served at room temperature! Is this what you call beer? Very much so, and it has a most honourable tradition. It is a good bet that British ales, together with the Belgian monastery beers, are closest to the beverage Europeans were drinking two or three hundred years ago, before the invention of the bottom-fermentation process and the lager-type beers that resulted. Traditionally, ale is brewed by top fermentation, is more or less hoppy in taste, and has a moderate alcohol content of between 3.5 and 6 percent ABV. Stronger beers are termed 'barley wines'. The primary purpose of an ale is to quench the drinker's thirst, be he Kentish farmer or Liverpool docker. For many years the common man's drink, ale is now perceived more as a top-of-the-range product, as if the British had at last become aware of the unique value of their national beer.

With the exception of a few bottled brands intended more for export than

for local consumption, ale is available almost exclusively on draught. But it comes in two quite distinct forms. On the one hand, there are 'cask' ales, nowadays more likely to come in metal than in wooden barrels. The beer they contain has had yeast added to it, so that the fermentation process continues after delivery to the pub. This demands real skill on the landlord's part, since he has to monitor and choose just the right moment to serve the beer, whose character is changing from day to day. The experienced drinker can therefore discern differences in the taste of a beer as between one pub and another, and even between one cask and another. Cask-conditioned beer is virtually impossible to standardise.

On the other hand, there are 'keg' ales, which have been kept in cool conditions

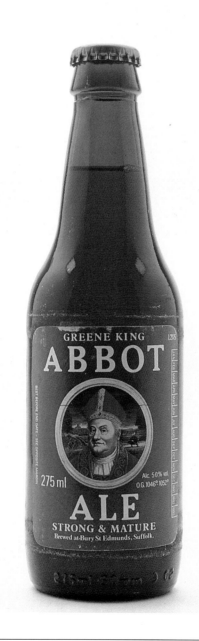

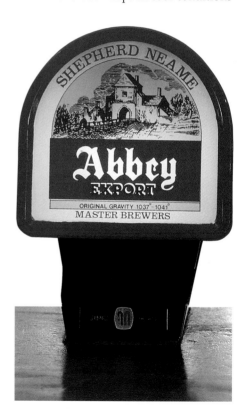

and had the yeast filtered out. One brewer's keg ale is therefore very similar in character to that of another. The watchword is convenience: the process enables modern brewers to offer a standardised product, regardless of time and place, even if it is not what the more discerning beer drinkers are looking for.

In the matter of taste, the use of wooden casks and the care required in the way it is served, a 'real ale' is in fact far more akin to a wine. It is therefore no surprise to learn that the British are just as particular about their ales as about a good claret or a fine sherry. When fully mature, an ale is served at cellar temperature (roughly 12 to 14°C), and

HOPS WITH A DIFFERENCE

British brewing is also unique in its approach to hops. Whereas elsewhere in the world only female hops are grown, the British have continued to use the male flowers, which they find eminently suitable for brewing ales. Among the best are the Fuggles and Goldings varieties, grown in Kent. The fact remains that, if bottom-fermentation beers gain further ground, the male hop will be under threat, since it is not so satisfactory for brewing lagers.

since it is not improved by the influence of carbon dioxide, every pint has to be pulled manually by the barman.

Once broached, a cask of ale must be drunk within twenty-four hours, since it deteriorates rapidly on contact with the oxygen in the atmosphere. Some brewers have tried to solve this problem by replacing the liquid drawn off with a blanket of CO_2, but this has not been popular with all drinkers. In any case, in most pubs it would be unusual if a cask of ale were not consumed before the bell announcing drinking-up time!

Cask-conditioned real ales were just too much trouble for the major British brewers, and twenty years ago they tried to replace them with the more stable keg beers. The manoeuvre provoked a general outcry, and led to the creation of CAMRA (Campaign for Real Ale), which was well supported by the press. In the late 1970s, this consumers' association took issue with the closing down of small breweries, to the point of organising funeral processions to mourn their demise. CAMRA also publishes an annual review, the *Good Beer Guide* (with a more frequent London edition). It lists some 5,000 British pubs (out of a total of 70,000) which make a point of serving real ales. Its annual summer festival is also a great opportunity for serious drinkers to get together and exchange information.

Twenty years on, things have settled down, with the big brewers making concessions to the demand for real ales, and small independent breweries finding a new lease of life. Many pubs have specialised in real ales, proudly displaying a list of the varieties they serve, often on blackboards.

In addition, over a hundred 'home-breweries' or 'pub-breweries' have been established, in some cases serving old styles of beer – porter, for example – that had all but disappeared.

The principal types of ale – pale, mild and bitter – differ mainly in their degree of bitterness, and sometimes in density. But these categories are by no means absolute, and each ale must be appreciated on its own merits as the expression of a particular region and the skills of the brewer concerned.

Although real ales have restored pride to British brewing, you need only visit a few pubs to realise that, alongside the traditional (and generally magnificent) pumps used for pulling pints of ale, it is now common to find draught outlets for 'continental' lagers, often served chilled. There is a growing demand for national brands like Carling (produced at the Bass brewery, though it originated in Canada) and for international pilsners such as Heineken, Foster or Stella Artois, a brand which in the last ten years has made a considerable impact, especially in London. Draught cider, too, has achieved considerable

popularity. There is no real danger that traditional ales will be supplanted, but even the splendid isolation of the British no longer seems immune to the major world trends in beer drinking. Though first brewed in Britain as far back as 1880, lagers were for many years only of minority interest. This is no longer the case today.

ALE OR BEER

Until the 17th century, when the practice of flavouring beer with hops was introduced from Flanders, British ale was flavoured chiefly with rosemary, a plant with the magical property of warding off evil spirits. This explains its importance in the many festivals – religious and secular – that relieved the tedium of daily life. The new style of beer was not an immediate success, and only when it took over the name of ale was it finally accepted everywhere. Ever since, the term 'ale' has been used to describe traditional beers, while the more general word 'beer' is used to refer to all barley-derived drinks. An Englishman would never dream of ordering 'a beer' in a pub. Even if he does not mention the brand, he will always ask for a particular type of beer: ale, bitter, mild, stout, or even lager!

PALE AND MILD ALES

As their name suggests, pale ales are straw-coloured beers made from lightly-roasted malt, distinctly hoppy in taste, whereas milds are a darker amber colour, low in alcohol (under 4 percent ABV) and sometimes sweetened by the addition of sugar. These are not absolute distinctions, however. In the view of authorities such as Christian Berger (author of *le Livre de l'amateur de bière – the Beer Drinker's Guide*), some pale ales should more accurately be classed as milds. The fact is that brewers are free to describe their beers as they see fit.

In any case, the British beer drinker is clearly not very concerned. He will tend to stick to one of the two or three beers dispensed at his favourite pub. Some will not even have a specific label, being known simply as 'Liverpool beer' or 'Leicester beer'.

The six big brewing concerns – Bass, Allied Breweries, Whitbread, Watney, Courage, Scottish & Newcastle – each offer a range of beers, produced at some seventy different breweries, mainly for regional distribution. Few of these, apart maybe from some Bass, Whitbread and Courage products, are drunk nationwide, despite the brewers' impressive networks of tied houses.

The difference between bottled and cask beers is most obvious in the case of pale ales, since the volume of CO_2 dissolved in the bottled version is necessarily greater. With admirable logic, British brewers often give different names to their ale according to its conditioning:

for instance, Worthington White Shield, a beer left to mature in the bottle, is a close relation of cask-conditioned Draught Bass.

Bass Pale Ale, Britain's oldest registered brand, bearing a distinctive red triangle, features in a famous painting by Manet, *Un bar aux Folies-Bergères* (1882), alongside bottles of champagne. Another popular pale ale, Double Diamond, is manufactured by Allied Breweries, one of the major national groups, whose antecedents can be traced back to the time of Richard the Lionheart and the Crusades. Burton upon Trent, the real

centre of pale ale brewing (London specialises in bitter), has long been famous for a particular manufacturing process known as Burton Unions. Whereas elsewhere the fermenting beer is carefully retained in its vat, open or closed as the case may be, in the Burton Unions system the fermenting wort is allowed to circulate from one vat to another, impelled by its own turbulence. This long and complex method has been abandoned by the big brewers and is now used only by the independent Marston brewery for its Pedigree Bitter. Another small town famed for its pale ales, Tadcaster in Yorkshire, boasts no less then three breweries: Bass, Courage and the independent Samuel Smith. Founded in 1758, Smith's brewery still uses another traditional system, the Yorkshire Square, an open fermentation tank whose walls are lined with large slabs of slate. More recent versions are made of steel. The beers produced by this method have a distinctly malty flavour.

The designation IPA (India Pale Ale) is a throwback to imperial days. So that their beers remained stable during the long sea journey to the colonies, brewers produced versions with plenty of hops. This ensured that fermentation continued during the voyage, obviating the risk of infection. Bass-Charrington still produce an IPA at Burton.

Slightly different from other pale ales, the Courage group's Bulldog, exported in bottled form as Martin's Pale Ale, has a higher alcohol content. Another example – from the same

brewer – of how difficult it is to define British ales with any real precision is Courage's Strong Pale Ale: amber in colour and hoppy in taste, it has much in common with a bitter. The Suffolk brewer Adnams produces another distinctive line in pale ales: the hoppy, bottle-conditioned Champion, with an alcoholic strength of just 3.1 percent, and the much stronger Broadside (ABV 6.3 percent), rich and full bodied, which also comes in bottles. The draught version does not exceed 4.4 percent.

Although London is known mainly for its bitters, some pubs nevertheless serve a mild brewed by Fullers. This independent brewer also produces a complex, well-balanced beer know as London Pride. Though designated a pale ale, it is far more akin to a bitter.

Mild is the speciality of the Midlands and the Manchester region. It is normally a great deal less bitter

than pale ale and of relatively low density. It is surprising that the great working-class centres of the North should have opted for such sweet beers, while Londoners have always preferred more bitter brews to quench their thirst. Milds are generally darker than other ales.

Of the milds distributed by independent brewers, it is worth noting Everards Mild, produced near Leicester, unusual in forming a generous head; Darley's Dark Mild, from Doncaster; Thwaites' Real Best Mild, a particularly dark beer, brewed in Lancashire; Fuller's Mild, from London; and Banks's, brewed at Wolverhampton (the related Hanson's Mild is also now produced in Wolverhampton, following the closure of Banks's Dudley brewery). The small Highgate brewery, a member of the Bass group, produces only mild ales.

Despite the efforts of CAMRA, mild ales seem to be in decline, with public tastes veering towards more bitter styles of beer. The bottled version of mild, known as brown ale, is slightly different. It

should not be confused with the rather sugary 'brown ale' of the South of England, which is a dessert beer.

This round-up of pale and mild ales, though far from complete, proves beyond doubt that there is no hard and fast borderline between different categories of ale. An interesting exercise is to compare the products of a particular brewer and find out what really distinguishes them. It is quite likely that if you then try ales with the same designations produced by one of his rivals, you will find that they do not match. A comparison of this kind shows that beer is primarily the affair of the brewer, to the chagrin of the marketing man, who would very much prefer to work with easily-defined products rather than let the beer speak for itself.

BITTER

Bitters are nowadays the most popular ales in Britain, where they account for three quarters of total beer consumption. Many pubs feature two versions, of different alcoholic strengths. The key to a bitter is its taste: the very

YOUNG'S, AN INDEPENDENT LONDON BREWER

Young's brewery was founded at Wandsworth in 1831 by Charles Allen Young on the site of the Ram, a much older establishment dating from the 17th century. Young's has remained proudly independent over the years and John Young, who has headed the firm since 1962, represents the fourth generation of his family.

Young's has specialised in fine bitters, its two great classics being Ordinary and the slightly stronger Special. The brewery also produces bottle-conditioned beers for export, for instance its Strong Export Bitter. The company has a superb network of pubs, including some of London's oldest and finest. Pride of place must go to *The Lamb* in Bloomsbury, where the bar is still equipped with revolving opaque glass screens dating from the Victorian era. Known as *snob screens*, these allowed gentlemen to cut themselves off from the rest of the company when they wanted to have a surreptitious drink with young ladies of easy virtue. A lamb is also the symbol of the Young brewery.

first sip diffuses the unmistakable spicy bitterness of hops. The colour may vary, from golden yellow through tawny to old gold. The alcohol content is relatively low, at least in the case of the commoner and less expensive 'ordinary' brews.

Bitter is proof, if proof were needed, of the high degree of expertise attained to

by the British brewing industry. To produce beers of such taste and complexity – beers which linger so satisfactorily on the palate – with at the same time so low an alcoholic strength and density, is no mean achievement. It is easy to produce strong-tasting beers by using quantities of malt to obtain a high alcohol content. But whereas common-or-garden brewers can produce only 'small beer' of little

interest at between 3 and 4 percent ABV, British ale brewers achieve truly magnificent results. Much of the credit must go to the top-fermentation process, though it has to be admitted that the Germans brew some fine bottom-fermentation pilsner beers of similar strength and density.

As in the case of other ales, the character of bitter varies quite considerably from one area of Britain to another.

Kent, where large quantities of hops are grown, offers some magnificent examples, such as Master Brew, from the Shepherd Neame brewery at Faversham. Shepherd Neame has been brewing beer continuously since 1698, longer than any other brewer in the land. In fact, the little town of Faversham boasts vestiges of a brewing industry going back to 1147! Shepherd Neame's other products include a Best Bitter; an Abbey Export, which is conditioned in smaller casks; and Pilgrim, a bottle-conditioned bitter with an alcohol content of less than 1 percent ABV. To meet a growing demand, the brewery also produces under licence lagers belonging to the Swiss Hürlimann group.

Living so near to Kent, Londoners have developed a marked taste for bitter. The capital has two long-standing breweries: Young's, whose Special Bitter is

renowned for its hoppiness, even more pronounced in the bottled export version; and Fuller's, who produce Chiswick Bitter, an E.S.B. (Extra Special Bitter) and the complex-tasting London Pride.

There are also some strong, full-bodied bitters, for instance XXXB, a distinguished beer produced by the Lincolnshire brewer George Bateman. In the East of England again, Adnams offer a very popular bitter, with an alcoholic content of just 3.6 percent.

Boddingtons is the traditional bitter of the Manchester region. The nearby Lees brewery produces Britain's strongest bitter, which weighs in at a fraction over 10 percent. Mitchell's of Lancaster also brew an E.S.B., the bottled version of which differs little from its draught counterpart.

Down in the southwest, in Dorchester, Eldridge Pope produce a slightly sweet Country Bitter, while the company's Royal Oak (ABV 5 percent) is one of the very few bottled bitters with a big export market.

Other bitters deserving a mention are Badger, also produced in Dorset by the Hall & Woodhouse brewery; 6X, from Devizes in Wiltshire; S.A., brewed at Brain near Cardiff; and many others. As Michael Jackson has observed: 'To explain the individualism of the French, General De Gaulle cited the example of cheese, claiming that no one could lead

a nation producing 265 different varieties. Great Britain produces roughly the same number of bitter ales.' Does this make the United Kingdom ungovernable? Be that as it may, bitter – like the Royal Family – is indissolubly linked with the British Isles.

THE PUB

A national institution on a par with the Monarchy, Britain's 70,000 or so public houses are as essential to the enjoyment of beer as the brewers themselves. Most are in fact owned directly by the breweries, though this ancient system is now feeling the wind of change.

Despite a relaxing of restrictions in recent years, pub opening hours are still a source of wonder to the foreign visitor: most pubs open at 11 a.m., close in the afternoon (except in London and a few other major cities), then reopen in the evening until 11 p.m. This system, introduced in the Victorian era as part of the war on alcoholism, is the equivalent of Prohibition in the United States or the legislation restricting the sale of alcoholic drinks in French cafés.

The business of a pub revolves around beer, with food and other drinks playing only a secondary role. On entering the rather plain public bar, or the more comfortable lounge, one is immediately struck by the magnificent manual beer pumps. With the handles made of wood or decorated china, they bear clips indicating the types of beer served by the establishment. Manual pumps of this kind dispense ale by mechanical pressure, requiring the barman to exercise his biceps two or three times on the handle in order to draw a pint.

Lagers are also served nowadays. Some are brewed in England, like Bass's Carling brand. Of the imported lagers, the leaders are Heineken and especially Stella Artois, which is making an enviable impact on the market. Cider, often on draught, is also available everywhere, as is white wine. The remainder of the trade consists of spirits and fruit juices.

Drinks are ordered at the bar and paid for on the spot. The visitor is then free to sit anywhere and stay as long as he pleases. This way of doing things creates a remarkable sense of conviviality. People quickly feel at home in a pub, engaging in friendly discussion even if they have never met before.

The British often have a pub lunch of sandwiches and salad. Some pubs put on a wide range of cooked dishes, but do not expect haute cuisine: the food is generally good, plain fare, at affordable prices.

Some pubs are of great antiquity and most are magnificently decorated, especially in London and the North of England. Pub signs with their incongruous and poetic names are an endless source of fascination: *The Fox and Anchor, The King's Head and Eight Bells, The Bunch of Grapes, The Fisherman's Cottage, The Burning Bush, The Hare and Hounds, The White Bear, The Ship in Dock*, and so on.

The Lamb, *London (top left)*,
The Roebuck, *Burton (bottom left and top right)*,
The Star Tavern, *London (bottom right): three examples of pubs with distinguished facades and interiors. Britain has many thousands of such treasures.*

STOUTS, PORTERS AND OLD ALES

British ale – of such antiquity that no one really knows when it was first produced – has survived the vagaries of time and fashion and is still the country's most popular type of beer. The same cannot be said of porter, a beverage with a fascinating history. Born in the early years of the Industrial Revolution, it rose to prominence in the nineteenth century, then went into decline and all but disappeared after the Second World War. True, it survives in the form of stout, whether British or Irish, but stout is not quite the same as porter.

Porter was supposedly invented by a certain Ralph Harwood, who first brewed it in London around 1720. According to historians (Michael Jackson in particular), Harwood had the idea of cashing in on a fashion that had caught on in the London pubs of his day. Drinkers would ask for a mix of all the beers available: pale, mild and brown ales. This combination was baptised 'Entire', a name still found in some advertisements (Entire Porter). The resulting beer was very dark and

fairly strong. Harwood decided to brew one beer that would replicate all three. It seems that porter was a very dense drink with a high alcohol content, though it varied enormously due to the lack of precision of the measuring instruments then available (if used at all). The barley (which may or may not have been malted) was roasted for a long time, and the beer brewed using top-fermenting yeasts.

Harwood's brew house – more akin to the micro-breweries that have emerged recently than to a brewery in the modern sense – was in the vicinity of London's great markets. The name of his beer quite likely derived from the market porters of the area, who

adopted it as their favourite tipple. Other, larger breweries soon followed Harwood's lead. For instance, Samuel Whitbread, who in 1742 founded the company that still bears his name, began to specialise in porter, though today it has been completely abandoned by his successors. Porter was allowed to mature for a relatively long period, in tuns that could be quite enormous. In the *Great British Beer Book*, Roger Protz tells the tale of a tun built by the Meux brewery so large that two hundred guests could eat a meal inside. A thick, nourishing beer, porter was primarily the drink of the London labouring classes, its development keeping pace with the industrialisation of the world's first modern capital city. Its decline, which set in at the beginning of the century, may have been due to rising taxes on strong beers. This paved the way for the lighter ales to make a comeback. This cannot be the whole story, however, as it does not explain why stout – porter's younger brother – was able to survive and maintain its popularity.

The might of the British Empire is undoubtedly the reason for London porter's fame in other parts of the world, where brewers soon imitated the style. There are still porters, in name at least, in Denmark, the Baltic countries and even in the United States and Asia.

It is to the credit of the modern micro-breweries that a few porters are still brewed in London, though they are not nearly as strong as the porters of the last century. Of the traditional brewers, Samuel Smith of Tadcaster in the

northeast is one of the very few still producing a porter. Known as Taddy, it is also obtainable in bottled form. Keeper of old traditions, the Samuel Smith brewery still employs a team of coopers, since its beers are fermented and matured in wooden barrels.

Even non-specialists can easily tell a porter from a stout: just place a full glass in front of a light source. Porter emits a slightly reddish halo, whereas a

stout will remain completely black and opaque.

Stout itself varies considerably in taste. The best known is, of course, the Irish stout popularised by Guinness, very dry and fairly bitter on the palate. In England, this style is often referred to as extra stout or dry stout. But England also has stouts of a quite different kind, a great deal sweeter, with a pronounced hint of chocolate. These sweet stouts were formerly known as milk stouts, until this name was banned lest it should mislead the customer. In fact, there was nothing deceptive about the name, since during manufacture the brewers add lactose, the sugar naturally found in milk. But for its alcohol content – and even that is not very high – it could almost be served as a soft drink for children.

The most widely drunk stout of this type is Mackeson, produced by the Whitbread group at its various breweries. The brewery where it originated, in Kent, specialised in this product in the 1930s, before it was taken over. A score of different milk stouts are obtainable in Britain, including the Scottish brewer Tennant's Sweetheart and Watney's Cream Label. Sweet stouts of this type are also popular in the former British colonies, particularly in the West Indies, where they are slightly stronger.

The other quintessentially English stout is the 'imperial' variety. Continuing the traditions of Empire, these creamy beers have a dominant caramel flavour

44

and are very strong. Courage's Imperial Stout, for instance, is in excess of 10 percent ABV, while Samuel Smith's is over 8 percent. This is explained by the fact that they had to make the long journey to the British colonies and, before the days of pasteurisation, their high density was a way of ensuring that they did not deteriorate en route. They were also known as Russian stouts, no doubt due to the popularity they enjoyed during the last century in Czarist Russia.

Whereas ales are primarily thirst-quenching drinks (which is not to detract from their flavour), English stouts are to be supped more slowly, demanding time and tranquility if they are to be appreciated in all their fullness.

This is also true of other British beers which, though less popular, are well worth trying. Sometimes known as 'dessert beer', traditional brown ale is

readily identified by its sweet flavour, obtained by allowing the sugars to caramelise slowly while the wort is cooking. It is a fairly dark brown beer, though not particularly strong, and with only the faintest hint of bitterness. Notable examples are produced by Watney's – Mann's Brown Ale – and by the King & Barnes brewery, at Horsham in Sussex. The place of this sweet type of brown ale is, however, being gradually usurped by a dryer variety produced in the northeast of England. The most popular is produced at the Newcastle brewery (now part of the Scottish & Newcastle group). Amber in colour rather than a true brown, it is transparent, with a distinctly malty flavour, and keeps well in bottles.

Several brewers still offer brown ales, for instance the unmistakable Strong Brown Ale produced by Samuel Smith; Double Maxim, brewed by Vaux of

Sunderland; or Newquay, from Redruth in Cornwall. Though this brown is labelled Steam Beer – a reference to the famous Californian product – the term has nothing to do with the brewing process.

Ale can also be aged, in which case it acquires the generic designation of old ale. The aging process can be as long as one or two years, as in the case of Strong Suffolk, occasionally produced by Greene King. The method bears

some resemblance to that used in brewing Belgian Rodenbach beers, in that the ale is blended with a younger brown beer after maturing in casks. This is undoubtedly a throwback to an older way of brewing and storing beer, since this process makes it possible to keep beer longer during the hot season. British brewers do not produce many long-maturing ales of this kind, though some are marketed for limited periods, particularly in winter. A good example is Winter Warmer, produced by the London brewer Young's, which is available from November to February in some of the best pubs. Old ales are often characterised by their fruitiness, for instance the excellent Old Peculier (now brewed by the Scottish & Newcastle group). Owd Rodger, from the Marston brewery, also deserves a mention.

The most famous is undoubtedly Thomas Hardy's Ale, brewed by Eldridge Pope of Dorchester. Being bottle conditioned, a great deal is exported. With an alcohol content of over 12 percent, it is also Britain's strongest beer. Thomas Hardy's was first brewed in 1968, to commemorate the fortieth anniversary of the death of a writer who did much to make Dorchester and its beers famous. The ale undergoes a third fermentation in the bottle (each bottle bears a serial number and the year of manufacture). The brewer recommends that it should not be opened for at least five years, and guarantees its drinkability for up to twenty-five. The beer matures with the passage of time, and connoisseurs take pleasure in discussing the character of the different vintages.

Another ale that ages well in bottles is

the Prize Old Ale brewed by Gale's of Portsmouth, also a beer of great strength.

These last two beers could equally be called barley wines, a term often used to describe the strongest British ales. But, as the reader will already have realised, the British are hardly meticulous in the way they ascribe names to their beers. The name 'barley wine' clearly derives from the almost winey character that certain strong ales

can take on with age. They will have an alcoholic strength of at least 6 or 7 percent ABV and may register 10 percent or over. Nowadays, they are a speciality of the independent brewers, who produce original styles of beer as a way of distinguishing themselves from the big nationals.

Some examples are Bishop's Tipple, one of the less strong examples, brewed by Gibbs Mew of Salisbury; or Tally-Ho, a beer redolent of the hunting field, marketed by Adnams of Southwold,

Suffolk, over the Christmas season. This brewery, whose roots go back to 1641, takes pride in delivering its beers (a range of ten or so) on traditional drays pulled by Percherons.

The two surviving London brewers each produce a barley wine: Young's dark and syrupy Old Nick (complete with portrait of the devil on the label), and Fuller's Golden Pride. But the national brewers have not completely abandoned the field: Whitbread

markets a well-known barley wine called Gold Label; Bass has its own version; and Watney produces Stingo.

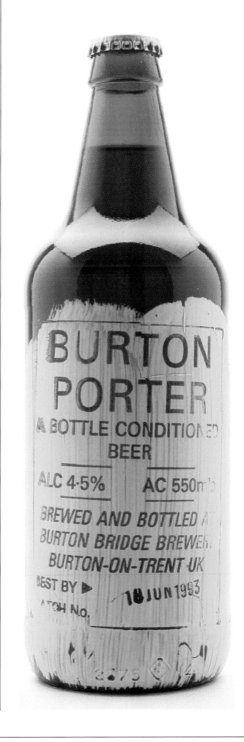

SCOTLAND

Known worldwide as the home of whisky, Scotland can also be proud of its beers, which are generally stronger and darker than elsewhere in Britain. The harsher northern climate undoubtedly has something to do with it.

Scotch ales are characterised first of all by their dark-brown, almost black colour, then by a greater density than the average British beer. Malty in taste, they are categorised as light, heavy, export and strong, ranging from 3 to 7 percent ABV. For many years, the Scots used a different classification, based on an ancient system of taxation expressed in shillings per barrel: 60/-, 70/-, 80/- and 90/-. This method of describing the strength of a beer in monetary terms is quite unique. Of course, the name has nothing to do with the price you pay for your pint.

Selling under the McEwans and Younger labels, the Scottish & Newcastle group is the chief brewer of Scotch ales. Similar beers with a predominant caramel flavour are also found in Belgium and the rest of Europe, but are generally stronger. Despite the tartan background and thistle emblem on the label, Gordon Ale is not uniquely Scottish, significant quantities being brewed in Belgium. But it is still an outstanding beer.

Of the other big nationals, Bass-Charrington (who brew mainly lagers under the Tennant label) and Watney also have plants in Edinburgh, which remains the centre of the Scottish brewing industry. The Sunderland-based Vaux group owns the Lorimer brewery, famous for its draught ale.

Scotland also has its independent brewers. Top of the list must come Caledonian, of Edinburgh, which regained its freedom after a management buy-out in 1987. 'A living, working museum of beer making', it still uses direct-fired open coppers to produce a wide range of malty-flavoured beers. These include a Strong Ale in excess of 7 percent ABV.

In the port of Dunbar, the Belhaven brewery, founded in 1719, also produces a fine assortment of Scottish ales. Though it supplies mainly draught beers, it also

BEER AND WHISKY

Equally beloved of the Scots, beer and whisky are more closely related than is generally recognised. Both derive from the same raw material – malted barley – and in both cases the purity of the water used is a vital factor in the quality of the end product. Moreover, the first stage in the production process -steeping the malt in water – is identical. Only then do the processes differ: beer is fermented, while whisky is distilled. Although the two products are kept quite distinct in Scotland, an enterprising French brewer, the Pêcheur group of Alsace, has had the idea of brewing a beer from peat-smoked malt, as used in whisky production. The result, an amber-coloured beer known as Adelscott, is achieving enviable sales figures.

markets Belhaven Scottish Ale, a bottle-conditioned version for export, which is amber coloured and highly carbonated. Lovers of Scottish castles will not be able to resist the appeal of Traquair House, owned by a laird of genuine Stuart extraction, who renewed the family tradition of brewing at the ancestral castle of Innerleithen in 1965. Fermented in great wooden tuns, his stronger beers cry out to be tasted before the magnificent open fire, like vintage port. And take a trip to Alloa, a small port not far from Edinburgh, to taste the typically Scottish ales of the Maclay & Co., one of Scotland's small independent brewers. Whilst in Scotland, the traveller will also come across a growing number of micro-breweries offering some most interesting beers. Though not yet as common as whisky distilleries, they are well worth a visit.

A LAND OF MICRO-BREWERIES

CAMRA's twenty-year campaign to safeguard traditional ales has generated a new interest in beer. This in turn has spawned a proliferation of micro-breweries, or brew-pubs, which brew beers for consumption on the premises. There are more than a hundred of them at the present time. Throwback to an ancient tradition – when the first secular breweries began by selling their wares in rooms at the front of the brew-house – these establishments often supply a range of five or six different beers, not to mention seasonal beers available at Christmas or in the summer.

In London, for instance, the ten-year-old *Orange Brewery* in Pimlico, its facade decorated with hop cones, sells two basic beers, humorously designated SW1 and SW2. It also serves a porter and a lighter beer, and special seasonal brews. Guest beers -in cask and bottle – are also on sale, but seem to make little impression on sales of the house ales. Go in the morning if you want to watch the brewing operations.

Burton-upon-Trent, ale capital and home of the giant Bass group, also boasts a micro-brewery, the *Burton Bridge*. It serves four regular draught ales, including a porter and a stout, and a number of seasonal beers. The rather small and stuffy bar is reached via a passageway along which waft the rich aromas of fermenting worts. You can buy the house porter in characteristic local bottles.

A number of the micro-breweries opened in recent times have taken advice from Peter Austin, formerly employed as a brewing engineer, who has founded his own brewery at Ringwood in Hampshire.

Facing page: The Orange Brewery, *in the Pimlico district of London, which has been in business for ten years.* Right, *beer pumps at the Burton Bridge micro-brewery at Burton upon Trent, high place of British brewing.*

IRELAND

Although the Irish may not have invented stout, they deserve the thanks of all beer drinkers for having made it known way beyond their own shores. For beer exports, Ireland is in fact one of the leading European nations.

Much of the credit must, of course, go to Guinness, an international group with interests in whisky, spirits and even champagne (subsequent to recent agreements with Moët et Chandon). Where beer is concerned, Guinness controls a string of fifteen or so breweries worldwide, and has its beers brewed under licence in some thirty others.

Like its precursor, porter, Irish stout owes its completely opaque black colour to the use of heavily roasted malts, which give it a unique toasty aroma. Dense without being too strong, stout is nowadays the drink that best exemplifies the ancient concept of 'liquid bread': sup a pint in one of Dublin's excellent pubs and you really feel you are feeding the inner man. Alas, this was often its function during the great famine that swept Ireland in the last century!

Arthur Guinness, founder of the world-famous brand, set up as a brewer in Dublin around 1760 and, like most of his contemporaries, began making the traditional ales. He was one of the first Irish brewers to produce a porter in the London style, and was so successful that he stopped brewing all other beers at the close of the eighteenth century. But it was his son, another Arthur, who in 1824 began making a denser, more hoppy stout – a better quality beer intended to stimulate a flagging market. It was a success and, by the middle of the last century, the Saint James Gate brewery was the biggest in the world. It still forms a remarkable enclave in the heart of the Irish capital, and its museum should be visited by every self-respecting lover of beer.

Despite the ubiquitous black and gold emblem, creamy head and unmistakable colour, there have for many years been different versions of the famous stout, produced for different markets. We can distinguish at least five.

The real McCoy is the draught version served in pubs in Dublin and throughout Ireland. It is the lowest in alcohol content and, not needing to be pasteurised, has an incomparable fresh mildness.

Known as Extra Stout, the Guinness sold in bottled form in Ireland and Great Britain is also a great drink. It undergoes a secondary fermentation in the bottle, which brings out all the flavour of the hops. Nor is it pasteurised.

This is unfortunately not the case with the draught Guinness sold in British pubs and elsewhere round the world. What a disappointment! It patently lacks the bouquet of the original. For anyone who has tasted the genuine article in a Dublin pub, this export Guinness can only be described as a poor imitation.

There is also a bottled version for export. It is slightly stronger than the original, not being subject to the bizarre Irish taxation system, which tends to restrict the density of beer.

Finally, for distant lands and hot climates, Guinness produces Foreign Extra Stout, a special version of even greater density. It is pasteurised to withstand long journeys and high temperatures.

The two other Irish stouts, Murphy's and Beamish, make much of their impeccable Irish pedigree, no doubt wanting to make the point that part of Guinness's production originates from a brewery in London.

Their pretensions are in fact somewhat hollow: Beamish, the older of the two (1792), and the more creamy, has belonged for the last thirty years to a Canadian group; Murphy's, whose stout is a lot more lively, is owned by Heineken.

It is also possible to find ales in the British tradition, Kilkenny (formerly Smithwick) being the most widely distributed, but they can hardly be said to be gaining ground. The real threat to Irish tradition comes from the ever deeper penetration of continental lagers, which are much appreciated by the younger generation. For them, stout is an 'old man's drink'. Guinness has fought back by producing its own lager, Harp, but surely the best solution would be to restore pride in Ireland's national tradition.

To show that they are not hostile to progress, Guinness and Murphy have recently introduced a new form of packaging for their stouts: a can containing its own tiny gas cartridge. When the beer is poured into the glass, the neutral gas causes a head to form, giving a good approximation of the dense cream that should grace any properly served Irish stout.

Serving draught Guinness is a skilled business. Unlike other beers, it cannot be 'hurried' by the use of carbon dioxide, but must be drawn slowly. To allow time for the head to form, the glass should be filled in two stages, or even in three. To ensure perfection, the wise will wait for a few minutes before beginning to sup. In any case, have you ever seen an Irishman in a hurry?

BELGIUM

Though relatively small in area, Belgium is a beer drinkers' paradise. Within its 30,000 sq. km. of territory, it produces every kind of beer known to man, including some found nowhere else, notably *gueuze* and *bière rouge*. There is an old Antwerp proverb to the effect that Belgium has three hundred and sixty different beers, one for each day of the year: the five remaining days are reserved for beers as yet uninvented!

Brussels can also boast the finest brewers' hall in the world. Built in 1551 and sited on the famous Grand-Place, it now houses the *Confédération des brasseries*. The number of breweries has declined greatly since the turn of the century, but the twenty or so still in production represent an impressive range of styles and tastes. Although beer is drunk mainly in the kingdom's 32,000 cafés, the quality of its bottled beers also makes Belgium the world's leading beer exporter.

In the land of Gambrinus and of Breughel, many of whose rustic scenes include foaming jugs of ale, beer is intimately bound up with the art of living.

Above: the Maison des Brasseurs, on the Grand-Place in Brussels, dates from 1551.
Left: Kermesse flamande *(Flemish country fair), by Brueghel the Younger (1564-1636). Musée de l'hôtel Sandelin, Saint-Omer.*

PILSNER BEERS

Pinte, chope, demi, bière or *canette*: the Belgians are certainly not short of words to describe their most popular beer. Pilsners – a type of lager – account for three-quarters of the 12 million hectolitres they consume each year.

Nowadays, production is extremely concentrated, with the two biggest brewing groups – Interbrew and Alken-Maes – between them representing four-fifths of all pilsner sales in Belgium.

Although these brewers have a long history, their lagers are of relatively recent origin. Interbrew, for instance, traces its roots back to 1366, when the Den Horen brewery was founded in Leuven (acquired by Sébastien Artois in 1717); but the well-known Stella Artois brand was not marketed until 1926. It was specially brewed for the Christmas festivities, which explains its name, the star symbol being popular with brewers worldwide. Jupiter, the Belgian market leader, also produced by the Interbrew group, comes from the Piedboeuf brewery at Jupille, renowned for the quality of its water. Artois and Piedboeuf joined forces in the late 1980s.

The only major group still operating its own malting, at Leuven, Interbrew is currently building two enormous, ultra-modern brewing plants to replace its existing installations. The group also produces other lagers: Loburg, intended to compete with more sophisticated beers of the Carlsberg or Tuborg type, and Lamot, a more regional product. It has expanded into the international market, with subsidiaries in France, the Netherlands, Italy, Hungary and Africa.

Belgium's second biggest brewer, Alken-Maes, is the result of a series of alliances and mergers. Alken, of Antwerp, and Maes, of Limburg province, both date

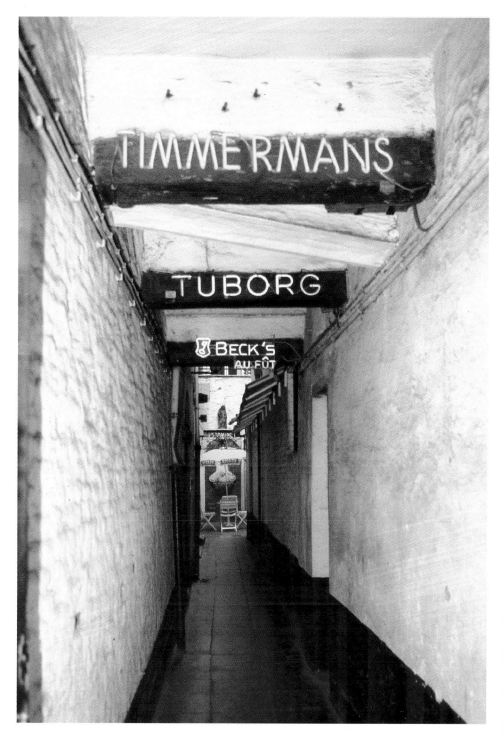

and Alken by the French giant Kronenbourg in 1978. In 1988, Maes separated from Watney, only to merge with Alken-Kronenbourg. This new combine owns two big brewing plants, one at Waarloos (Antwerp), the other at Alken. Haacht, the third-ranking Belgian brewer, whose Primus lager is also extremely popular, will celebrate its centenary in 1998. The brewery is located between Brussels and Malines. Haacht has remained independent, while showing a readiness to innovate: in 1986, for instance, it came up with the 'Quick bottle', a wide-necked container obviating the need for a bottle opener.

Although these major brands dominate the market, there is still room for at least fifty regional or local pilsners, sold direct to the consumer or, in draught form, through a small network of cafés.

Though known abroad mainly for the diversity and quality of its special beers, Belgium can be equally proud of its lagers. Drawing beer is a highly skilled occupation, and there is a major annual competition to find the best barmen. A specialist organisation – the Office national du débit de la bière -organises training courses and examinations in the skills of drawing and serving beer, awarding diplomas and plaques. Losing the sought-after ONDB rating is a real dishonour for a Belgian café proprietor.

Above, the 1991 winner of the award for the best Belgian barman.

from the last century and for many years went their separate ways. Cristal Alken, a pilsner beer derived directly from the Czech original, was first brewed in 1928, while Maes Pils, formulated with the help of a German brewer, made its debut in 1946.

The two breweries were both eventually bought out by foreign concerns: Maes by the British Watney-Mann group in 1969,

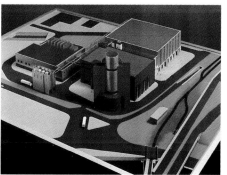

Left, a model of the new breweries under construction at Leuven.

TRAPPIST BEERS

Five Belgian abbeys (and a sixth in the Netherlands) have breweries on their premises and retain the exclusive right to use the 'trappist' designation for their beers (a right confirmed in 1962 by a verdict of the Ghent courts). The term also denotes a specific style of beer: top-fermented, made from dark malts, with a distinctly hoppy flavour. When it comes to bottling, the brewer adds some candy sugar and a dose of yeast, which induces a secondary fermentation and the formation of a deposit in the bottle. A trappist beer is therefore always kept upright and poured gently to avoid disturbing the sediment.

Although these beers evoke the great traditions of the medieval monasteries, they in fact have no historical continuity with medieval times. The ancient foundations were destroyed time and time again, and the present buildings date from no earlier than the 19th century. Each abbey has its own interpretation of the trappist formula, and in any case brews several distinct variants. The abbey of

Chimay, located in Hainault province, dates from 1850. It began brewing in 1860, and now produces more than 100,000 hectolitres a year. Its labels bear the distinctive lily emblem. Chimay Rouge is a smooth, sweet, amber-coloured beer (ABV 6.2 percent). Chimay Blanche (ABV 7 percent), on the other hand, is a great deal drier, to the point of astringency. The trio is completed by Chimay Bleue (ABV 8 percent), a strong beer that can be left to age (each bottle bears details of the vintage). Since the War, the Chimay brews have owed much to the personality of Father Théodore.

Orval, in Southern Belgium, not a stone's throw from the French frontier, has been the site of an abbey since 1070. The present buildings were begun in 1926, and it was to finance their completion that the monks set up a brewery in 1931, drawing water from an ancient spring – the *fontaine Mathilde* – which rises in the monastery grounds. Orval produces just one beer, ABV 5.2 percent. Hops are added when the wort is cold, giving the beer a distinctively bitter taste. The date of bottling is stated on the label.

Founded in 1230, the abbey of Notre-Dame-de-Saint-Rémy, near Rochefort in the province of Namur, was producing beer as far back as the 16th century, but solely for the personal needs of the monks. In modern times, the abbey has been brewing since 1907, though the present installations did not come on stream until 1960. Members of the public are not admitted, and the brewery functions strictly according to the rule of the order, the process beginning at half past three in the morning. Three beers are produced at Rochefort, with ABV ratings of of 6.2, 8 and 10 percent. All are deep amber in colour, with a remarkably complex flavour and powerful nose. They should be drunk at a temperature of 15 or 16 °C.

The abbey of Westvleteren, near Ypres in Flanders, dates from 1830 and has been brewing its own beers since 1938. But after the Second World War, in order not to disrupt the meditations of his monks, Father Gérardus decided to produce only enough beer to meet the needs of the community and to supply just one café – *De Vrede* – situated opposite the abbey. The monks nevertheless granted a licence to the nearby brewery of Saint-Bernard-de-Watou, which now produces and markets three trappist beers bearing the Saint-Sixtus label: Pater, Prior and Abt.

Founded in 1804 near Antwerp, the abbey of Westmalle began brewing in 1836. In 1870, it started marketing its growing output, in engraved bottles, to finance missions in the Congo.

The installations were entirely refurbished in 1934 and now produce two beers: Dubbel, deep-coloured (due to the use of dark-coloured sugar candy), with a strong malty flavour and creamy consistency; and the golden-blonde Trippel (made with white sugar candy). This is a complex beer, combining a slightly acid fruitiness with a high alcoholic content (ABV 9 percent).

ABBEY BEERS

Whereas 'trappist' beers are brewed on monastery premises by genuine monks (in some cases with assistance from lay personnel), abbey beers are all produced by private brewers and are more or less intimately associated with the monasteries whose names they bear.

Their common denominator is that all hark back to the medieval tradition of monastic brewing, and some even follow old recipes that have come to light again. But the historical continuity between the beers of yesteryear and their modern counterparts is often tenuous, apart from the basic technique of top fermentation.

Just as the present-day trappist fathers have only been brewing for at most a hundred years, often less – their monasteries having been in abeyance for decades or even centuries – abbey beers, too, are of recent origin, and many have been around for less than twenty years.

Why then have they scored such a resounding success? In our day and age, it is unlikely to have anything to do with the appeal of the contemplative life, particularly where beer drinkers are concerned! So we must look elsewhere to discover why a type of beer that had practically disappeared from Belgium between the Wars is now experiencing a revival. The explanation is simply an understandable reaction on the part of consumers to the omnipresence of bottom-fermentation lagers and their all-to-often

uniform taste. The revival in interest in abbey beers is evident in France and Italy, as well as in Belgium. Here is further evidence of the 'renaissance' in informed beer drinking preached over many years by the specialist writer Michael Jackson.

Of itself, the term 'abbey' does not really denote a particular class or style of beer, though such beers are generally brewed by top fermentation and are stronger than their run-of-the-mill counterparts. Extremely diverse, they range from pale to dark through all shades of amber; may undergo a double, and even a triple fermentation (generally in the bottle); and vary enormously in malt content and in bitterness. The fact remains that the drinker

is rarely disappointed by a beer with an abbey label, since the vast majority of Belgian brewers deploy all their skills to obtain flavoursome, full-bodied beers that will often linger on the palate.

Like their trappist rivals, abbey beers are often brewed in a range of strengths, colours and densities. For instance, there are no less than five beers bearing the label of the Abbaye de Leffe.

Abbey beers fit into one of two categories:

In some cases, existing monasteries have entered into a commercial agreement to allow their names and associated prestige to be exploited by a brewer, whether or not they have themselves brewed beer in the past. This is true of Affligem, Bonne Espérance, Bornem, Brogne, Floreffe, Grimbergen, Leffe, Maredsous, Tongerlo, Triple Val Dieu, Cambron, to name but some.

In other cases, brewers have taken up the names of long-abandoned monasteries or have invented a name with monastic overtones to give cachet to their special beers. Such is the case of Aulne, Corsendonk, Moinette, St Feuillien, St Benoît, Triple Moine, St Bernardus, Sanctus, Cuvée de l'Ermitage, Witkap Pater, Augustijn, and so on.

The history of the Abbaye de Leffe is quite typical in this respect. Its beers are among the oldest on the market and in terms of volume its production is second to none. It was fulsomely described as 'a worthy ambassador for Belgium' by the Belgian publication *Bière Magazine*, which in 1991 investigated beers of this kind in some depth.

The abbey itself is located in the south of Belgium, near Dinant, on the banks of the

Leffe, a modest tributary of the Meuse. It was founded at least as early as 1152 and is still occupied by a small community of Prémontré monks. There are historical documents to prove that the monks were drinking their own beer in 1240, but not until the 15th century did the monastery have its own brewery on the premises, the beer still being exclusively for the enjoyment of the inmates.

Over the centuries, the brewery buildings eventually succumbed, having suffered the ravages of flood, fire, war and pillage, although the monastery itself somehow managed to survive. The modern history of the place begins in 1954, when a lay brewer, Albert Lootvoet d'Overijse, was looking for a top-fermentation beer to add to his range. He came across the ancient recipes of the Leffe Abbey monks and, after signing a

contract with their successors, started producing the brew. Success smiled on him (the beer won the favour of Parisians as early as 1957), and soon the little brewery was no longer equal to the task. Operations were consequently transferred to Mont-Saint-Guibert in Brabant, and the firm was

SUGAR CANDY – A LINK WITH CHAMPAGNE

The addition of sugar candy to certain trappist and abbey beers at the moment of bottling is not unlike the process whereby champagne growers add syrup to their product after it has been uncorked and the sediment shot off. In brewing, too, the sugar –obtained in a special way by crystallizing beetroot juice – is not used as a sweetener but is intended to ferment, adding proteins and mineral salts to the beer. Besides their monastic origins, abbey beers and champagne have something in common in the way they are produced.

eventually taken over by the Interbrew group, which made Leffe the flagship of its special beers range.

There are now five different versions of Leffe beer: Blonde, the most popular (also available on draught), ABV 6.6 percent; the slightly less strong Brune (ABV 6.3 percent); Vielle Cuvée (ABV 7.8 percent), a beer flavoured with spices; Triple (ABV 8.4 percent), which undergoes a second fermentation in the bottle; and Radieuse (ABV 8.5 percent), the strongest of all and also the most highly hopped. Much of Leffe's production of over 400,000 hectolitres is exported, to as far afield as California! The monks are kept informed of the use made of the name of their abbey, particularly in advertising campaigns, and also have a representative on the company's board of management.

The French Revolution and the Napoleonic Wars led to the closure of many abbeys, in Belgium as well as in France. But these political upheavals do not, alone, explain why the monks gave up brewing. The fact is that, when they were again free to lead a monastic life, in the middle years of the nineteenth century, many monasteries did not return to brewing their own beers. The reason is explained by historian Marie-Anne Wilssens in her study of Grimbergen abbey. 'When, in 1847, the abbey was again restored to its original use, there was no

revival of brewing. From then on, abbey beers were produced by outside interests (...) The abbey had lost almost all the landed estates which might have supplied the raw materials, and organising a brewery was a costly enterprise. Also, there had been a general change in people's eating and drinking habits, to which abbeys were not

immune (...) The growth in population forced up the price of grain, and in turn occasioned a rise in the price of beer.'

Moreover, from the end of the 17th century, abbeys had to pay tax on the beer they consumed, a further disincentive to their continuing or recommencing brewing operations.

Another abbey of the Prémontré order, Grimbergen also dates from the Middle Ages. The phoenix of its emblem denotes that it was several times ravaged and the monks dispersed, but each time they returned to begin again. In 1956 the monks signed an agreement with the Maes brewery at Waerloos, granting Maes the right to brew beers to their traditional recipes, in particular Optimo Bruno, an extremely dense blond beer, famous in the region in the 17th and 18th centuries.

In 1978, the operation was transferred to the bigger Union brewery at Jumet, then Maes became part of the French BSN group, creating even more outlets for Grimbergen beers. There are four in all: Blonde (ABV 6.5 percent); Double, a dry brown beer, also with an alcohol content of 6.5 percent, which, as the name suggests, is made to ferment a second time; Triple (ABV 8 percent), a creamy beer, which undergoes a third fermentation in the bottle; and Optimo Bruno, the celebrated amber-

coloured liquid, which weighs in at 10 percent. The royalties paid to the abbey afford the monks freedom from financial worries, and are even sufficient to restore their buildings.

Another example of monastic continuity is the abbey of Maredsous, near Dinant. One of its former inmates was Father Attout, himself the son of a brewer, who around

1930 perfected the recipe for the community's own beers. In the post-war years, beer production was handed over to outside contractors, and for the last thirty years Maredsous beers have been produced by the Moortgat company, at Breendonk in Flanders. This brewery is also famous as the producer of Duvel (Flemish for Devil): an illustration of the way in which beer tends to break down barriers and sometimes brings together the most surprising bedfellows! There are several Maredsous varieties: 6°, a blond beer, which undergoes secondary fermentation in the bottle; 8°, a dark, filtered brown; 9°, a re-fermented brown beer; and 10°, a blond beer, which is also allowed to ferment a second time in the bottle.

There is no shortage of curiosities in Belgian brewing, and a single brewer may well produce two different abbey beers. This is the case of the Lefèvre de Quenast firm, which brews both the Bonne Espérance and Floreffe abbey beers. The former originates from a Prémontré monastery near Binche, an important architectural monument (particularly its 13th-century cloister), which nowadays houses a college of some 600 pupils. The idea of brewing a beer bearing the abbey name was suggested by the old boys' association, as a way of safeguarding the buildings and reviving the institution's cultural traditions. It is now produced by the Lefèvre brewery, after periods with two other brewers. A blond beer with an ABV rating of 8 percent, Bonne Espérance is enjoying great success, particularly in Italy.

Floreffe was also a Prémontré abbey and has a delightful mill-and-brewery complex dating from the Middle Ages. Brewing was revived in 1968, and since 1983 has been in the hands of Lefèvre. There are four different brews, but it is the blond version (ABV 6 percent), filtered and pasteurised, that accounts for the bulk of sales.

Not to be outdone, the De Smedt brewery at Opwijk undertakes to brew beers for a trio of abbeys: Affligem, Aulne and De Poster. In the case of Affligem (near Alost), the monks were brewing as far back as 1570 and, after the hiatus of the Revolution, continued to do so until 1950, when they finally placed the operation in lay hands. Since 1970, the three Affligem varieties – blond, brown and an ABV 8 percent Triple – have been produced by De Smedt.

Of Aulne abbey only the ruins remain, apart from the abbot's office, now a presbytery. But the name lives on in the form of a blond beer, and also a cheese. After a number of ups and downs, the Norbertine fathers of De Postel abbey near the Dutch border have also entrusted their brewing activities to De Smedt.

By way of contrast, the two varieties of a single abbey beer – Corsendonk – are produced by two different brewers, one in Flanders, the other in Wallonia. It is a truly Belgian tale, and instructive as to the development of the industry in Belgium. A priory existed at Corsendonk as early as 1398, and documents attest that it possessed an important brewery, together with a mill and malting – all swept away in the French Revolution. Not far away, at Turnhout near Antwerp, in 1906 Antonius Keersmaeker set up a brewery and began producing prize-winning beers. But brewing came to a halt in the 1950s. Thirty years later, Keersmaeker's great grandson, mindful of the revival of abbey beers, decided to brew one in honour of the ancient priory. However, he now lacked the necessary installations and, for technical reasons, had to entrust the brewing operations to two different concerns. Agnus, a blond beer with an ABV rating of 7.5 percent, is now produced by the Du Bocq brewery at Purnode; while Pater, a brown, is handled by Bios of Ertvelde (this firm also brews the Bornem and Tongerlo abbey beers). The two Corsendonk beers nevertheless come in similar distinctive packaging and are marketed as a single product.

Finally, just to show that in Belgium nothing is straightforward, one abbey beer is brewed in a lay brewery and sold exclusively in a monastery: the abbey of Cambron, near Mons, of which only an imposing tower now remains. Le Domaine, which manages the ancient building, asked the Silly brewery to produce a special amber-coloured beer with an alcohol content of 6 percent. It is sold exclusively on the premises, and in very limited quantity. Well worth a pilgrimage, don't you think?

WHITE BEERS

At one time very popular, so-called 'white' beers – i.e. beers which include wheat as well as barley in their composition – had all but died out earlier this century. Their characteristic cloudy appearance was less attractive to consumers than the crystal clarity of pilsner beers.

The Flemish-speaking part of Brabant

province (around Leuven) boasted dozens of white beers a century ago; reduced to two at the end of the Second World War. Originally, these beers were brewed mainly by farmers and were quite low in alcohol. Their unique flavour, slightly tart and very refreshing, was due to the use of wheat and oats with the malt, and to a secondary fermentation in the bottle. Brewed only in summer, white beers were known above all for their thirst-quenching properties, the result of their slightly acid composition.

We owe the revival of white beers to one man – Pierre Célis – and a small town – Hoegaarden, near Leuven. Dairyman and livestock merchant, Célis tells how, one summer evening in the 1960s, he was spending time with a few friends: 'One of them lamented the fact that one could no longer enjoy a good white beer as in the old days, and that never again would it be produced in Hoegaarden.' The last brewer had shut up shop just a few years before.

Living close to the former brewery, Pierre Célis had often watched white beer being made. He decided to try his hand at producing the stuff on a very small scale and asked advice of the last surviving brewer. Combining expertise from the

past and modern technology, he steadily increased his capacity, took on his first employee in 1975, obtained financial backing, and renamed his brewery De Kluis (The Hermitage). Following a fire at the brewery, he was forced to seek outside help and joined the Interbrew group, whilst remaining in complete control of the brewing and development of his product.

In the case of Hoegaarden white beer, success was not slow in coming: production had reached 400,000 hectolitres by 1991, after just twenty years of brewing. Thirst-quenching, fresh, low in alcohol, it appeals mainly to young people and to the ladies, especially during the hot summer months. It owes these properties to the use of wheat and oats, and also to the addition of certain spices (coriander, curaçao) as well as hops. Unfiltered, it maintains its milky, cloudy appearance.

The craze for Hoegaarden has inevitably stimulated other brewers into action. Since the 1980s, many other white beers have come onto the market, revivals of ancient brands or entirely new creations. They include Blanche de Bruges, from the De Gouden Boom brewery, first marketed in 1983; Riva Blanche, from Dentergems, 1985; Blanche d'Audenarde, 1987; Watou's, from the Van Eecke brewery, 1988; Steendonk, a joint effort by the Palm and Moortgaat breweries, 1989; Blanche Foudroyante of Brussels; and a host of others.

An exceptional case is the small Kroon brewery, near Leuven, which has been brewing white beer without a break since

WITH OR WITHOUT LEMON

From Germany, where the white beers are very different from their Belgian counterparts, comes the custom of putting a round of lemon in the glass to increase the acidity of the beer. This is frowned on by Belgian brewers, who maintain that their white beers are in no need of such expedients.

---

the 19th century, albeit in very limited quantities. Its Double Blanche has an alcohol content of 3.5 percent.

The success that Belgian white beers have met with abroad, particularly in France, is bound to encourage brewers to develop this sector, to the great delight of traditional beer enthusiasts.

SPECIALITY BEERS

Rather than a well-defined category, this is a collective term to describe the great diversity of unusual beers which only the imaginative Belgian brewers could have invented. If proof were needed that beer is a versatile drink, here it is, even if you feel that Delirium Tremens, its label decorated with diminutive pink elephants, goes beyond the bounds of beer-drinking decorum!

Although they are often high in alcohol and in some cases brewed by top fermentation, speciality beers respond as much to fashion and to marketing

considerations as to genuine local traditions. Nevertheless, Belgium still has many small or medium-sized breweries which have managed to maintain their independence in the face of the big boys by brewing original products with a strong local following. According to experts such as Michael Jackson, the existence and development of these strong beers owes much to the fact that sales of other spirits in Belgian cafés was banned in 1919. To satisfy the customers, the brewers responded by supplying beers stronger than the ubiquitous pilsners.

At Antwerp, for instance, the locals are still faithful to De Koninck, a beer served in the traditional stemmed goblet known as a *bolleke*. Brewed by the De Koninck and Van den Bogaert families for exactly one hundred and fifty years, De Koninck is a top-fermentation beer (ABV 5.1 percent), brewed using an original strain of yeast. In the beginning it was associated with an inn called *De plaisante Hof*, and for over a century the beer was conditioned only for draught consumption, in casks of 150, 75

and 37.5 litres. In fact, it was not available in bottled form until the 1950s and is still best drunk as a draught beer, especially since café proprietors do not use top pressure to dispense it, but rely on its naturally high carbon dioxide content. The brewery is also involved in an operation to

restore traditional Antwerp inns and taverns, such as *Het Vliegend Peerd*, dating from the 15th century, or the *'t Ekster* café

at Deurne, once frequented by the painter Brueghel. Despite the need to modernise its brewing plant, De Koninck has remained committed to producing a unique and truly flavoursome beer.

Another beer with a great tradition is Rodenbach, a *bière rouge* (red beer) from

the Flemish town of Roeselare. Also known as Bourgogne des Flandres (Flemish Burgundy) – though there is another brown beer sold under this label – it is unique of its kind, and its name may not be misappropriated. Produced by the same family for many generations, Rodenbach is a complex beer to brew:

using four types of malt and five different strains of yeast, the brewer blends a number of young and aged beers, before the maturation process proper. This stage lasts from eighteen months to two years and takes place in oak tuns – a method rarely used in brewing, since it is slow and costly. The storage vessels have to be renewed at regular intervals, and the brewery in fact employs its own team of coopers. When they have matured, Rodenbach, Grand Cru and Alexander beers are decanted into bottles, and sugar is sometimes added at this stage. Despite their age, they are remarkably fresh and the way the taste lingers is quite amazing. Beers to be savoured with the greatest respect, both draught and bottled versions are beginning to be found beyond the confines of Belgium.

There are a number of other *bières rouges* to be found in Flanders, but the maturation process is much shorter.

At Oudenaarde, also in Flanders, the

Liefmans brewery (founded 1679) produces some original brown beers somewhat reminiscent of English brews: top-fermenting yeasts are used, and the wort is simmered gently overnight. The resulting beer is kept in the bottle for up to two years in the case of the Goudenband

(Golden Ribbon) label. Managed for many years by Mrs Rose Blanquaert-Mercks, Liefmans is now part of the Riva group based in Dentergem, the leading producer of speciality beers. By buying out small independent firms likely to go under despite the quality of their beers, the Riva group provides better marketing channels, especially for exporting, whilst ensuring that the individual beers survive. In addition to its well-known white beer (see

previous section), brands now marketed by Riva include Lucifer, Carolus d'Or, Triple Toison d'Or and Straffe Hendrik.

Other brown beers not dissimilar in character are the Brune de Malines; Brune d'Audenarde, from the Felix brewery; Oud Zottegem, produced by Crombé; or even Carolus d'Or (Gouden Carolus), more like an ale, though it is left to mature for a year in the bottle at the brewery.

Among the stronger beers, one of special interest is Bush. It bears no relation to the light beer of that designation produced in the United States, but is simply the English translation of the name of the brewers, Dubuisson, a family hailing from Pipaix in Hainault province. The British allusion is justified, since this beer is very similar in character to a strong barley wine (ABV 12 percent), though the colour is a clear coppery red.

Another Belgian tradition that still goes on is the brewing of *bière de Saison*, originally a harvest-time drink, particularly thirst-quenching though not necessarily low in alcohol, since it may well have an ABV rating of 5 percent. Seasonal beers of this kind are pale amber or almost orange in colour. Some of the most typical are Régal, brewed by Du Bocq; Pipaix, by Bisset; and Silly.

LA CHEVALERIE DU FOURQUET

Taking as its motto 'Amitié et Servir' (Friendship and Service), the Chevalerie du Fourquet is the confraternity of Belgian brewers and has been in existence for over forty years. Its headquarters is the Maison des Brasseurs, in Brussels. It takes its name from the ancient, fork-like instrument used by brewers to stir the wort. Its main purpose is of course to honour all those who work to promote the nation's beers, by electing them to its ranks and granting diplomas. But its members have also carried out historical studies of brewing and of Saint Arnould and Gambrinus in particular, organise events featuring the country's beers, and help young people intending to work in the brewing and malting trades.

Of relatively recent origin, Double and Triple beers derive from the abbey style, having adopted the abbey fermentation techniques, whether in vat, cellar or bottle. Among the most widespread are Triple de Steenbrugge, Triple de Bruges, and the Triple Toison d'Or from Malines.

Links formed between Belgium and Britain during the two World Wars may explain the attraction felt by Belgian brewers for ales in the British tradition. Whatever the reason, there is no denying that many Belgian beers are more of less reminiscent of their English and Scottish counterparts, though generally slightly stronger.

Whilst on this subject, the history of the John Martin brewery is instructive. A master brewer born in Britain, John Martin settled in Antwerp in 1909, reckoning that Belgian drinkers were better able to appreciate the virtues of his beers than were his fellow countrymen. There he developed his speciality, the highly successful Martin's Pale Ale. He also introduced Guinness, then in 1924 created the Gordon brand, with its thistle emblem on a tartan background. Today, his three grandchildren continue the family tradition, brewing British-type beers with an authentic Belgian character. The John Martin brewery is moreover the chief patron of a number of typically Flemish folk festivals, such as the Fêtes des Chats at Ypres or the Carnaval des Blancs Moussis at Stavelot.

Winston, Gordon Scotch Ale, Op Ale or Vieux Temps, Ginder Ale, Spéciale Palm and Spéciale Aerts are other brands demonstrating the way in which Belgian brewers have drawn inspiration from British traditions.

At Hoegaarden, the success of the revived

white beer encouraged the De Kluis brewery to try its hand at other, stronger, products. These include its Grand Cru and Fruit Défendu, a beer to which spices other than hops are added, reviving a practice from the early Middle Ages.

Finally, Belgium has a number of quite unique special beers: the flavoursome Straffe Hendrik from Bruges; Gulden Draak in its stoneware bottle; Hapkin, bearing the axe emblem; Rétro; Houten Kop, reminiscent of the the beers brewed in Zeeland, Holland; Brigand, which comes in a champagne-type bottle with wired cork; Gauloise, fermented a second time in the bottle; and many more.

Other curiosities include a Napoleon beer, another labelled Gambrinus, and Kwak, a strongish amber beer which owes its success to an original glass: an hour-glass

shaped vessel supported by a small wooden stand.

There is even a beer without a brewery: Ciney. This little village is used as an emblem by the Demarche company, which has some excellent beers brewed to its own recipes by the Interbrew and Alken-Maes groups. Ciney is sold in three versions: Cuvée Brune, a racy Blonde and, more recently, Spéciale 10 with its magnificent blue-and-silver label. All are sipped from tiny, 12-centilitre glasses.

There is possibly only one general criticism to be made of Belgian brewing: a certain lack of openness and clarity. Often the label tells you nothing about the nature of the beer, its characteristics or place of origin. This can lead to an unfortunate lack of precision, with brewers tempted to produce beers under 'flags of convenience', with names which give the consumer no guidance as to what he is drinking.

BREW-IT-YOURSELF

If you still think the range of Belgian speciality beers is a bit limited, or would like to try out brewing techniques for yourself, there is a company making a whole range of beers in kit form, for you to brew at home. Under the name of Brewferm, Farma-Import markets wort preparations, from which 80 percent of the water has been evaporated. By adding hot water, yeasts and sugar, leaving the liquid to ferment for two weeks and keeping the resulting brew for a further six weeks in bottles, you can produce beers of your own. More than thirty different beers can be made in this way, ranging from pilsners to abbey beers and including many of the main Belgian styles. The technique (invented in the UK) does work, but it takes a certain amount of equipment and a great deal of care and attention (particularly in avoiding contamination) if you are to obtain decent results.

MUSEUMS OF THE BREWER'S ART

Not surprisingly, a great brewing nation such as Belgium has many museums devoted to the art, not least the collection housed in the Maison des Brasseurs, on

the Grand-Place in Brussels. The various exhibits illustrate how beer was brewed in the past, and there is a bar where visitors can sample beers, whose names are never revealed by the barman (different beers are served each week). In 1992, new rooms were opened featuring modern brewing techniques, including conical fermentation and maturation tanks.

Whilst stressing the nobility of the raw materials used in brewing, the museum also shows how information technology, filtration, chilling and bottling are nowadays key factors in successful brewing. A serious attempt has been made not to limit brewing to its historical past.

At Roumedenne in the province of Namur, the Musée européen de la

brasserie was the brainchild of Charles Fontaine de Gheslin, a great enthusiast who used the old Bouty brewery as a showcase for the thousands of publicity items he had collected. Unfortunately, the museum was forced to close down in early 1993.

Antwerp has its own brewers' confederation, housed in a Renaissance building with a fascinating history: the

Maison Hydraulique was formerly the water distribution centre for the city's breweries, and functioned well into the 20th century! All the installations are in perfect condition. There is also a small museum illustrating the old, small-scale brewing techniques.

Centre of Belgian hop growing, Poperinghe boasts the only European museum devoted exclusively to this

essential beer ingredient, with instruments, machines and a wealth of documentation. Every September at hop festival time, Poperinghe is the scene of a grand procession and lively celebrations. Also worth visiting are Leuven's municipal museum, headquarters of the leading Belgian brewing group; the Martens brewery at Bocholt; the local museum at Hoegaarden, capital of white

beer; and the open-air museum at Bokrijk, devoted to former agricultural occupations and crafts, where beer has its rightful place.

LUXEMBOURG: A TRADITION STRETCHING BACK NINE HUNDRED YEARS

Though a great deal less flamboyant than their Belgian cousins, the brewers of the Grand-Duchy of Luxembourg can nevertheless boast some deep-rooted traditions and a prestigious brewing history. The Mousel brewery can in fact claim to have existed since 1083, founding date of Altmunster abbey, with which it shares its site (in 1972, this establishment merged with the Clausen brewery and is now part of the Brasseries réunies de Luxembourg). In 1815, before bottom-fermentation pilsner beers swept (almost) all before them, Luxembourg had no less than four hundred small-scale breweries on its territory. By 1840, the number had fallen to twenty four.

A man who left an enduring mark on brewing in the Grand-Duchy was Henri Funck (b. 1775), and his descendents have enlivened many local societies. The Funck brewery was in the forefront of technological innovation (refrigeration equipment, storage cellars, steel tanks) for many decades, before finally being absorbed by the Brasseries réunies in 1982. Nowadays this group produces mainly pilsner beers, including the Mousel, Clausen and Funck brands, luxury beers (*bières de luxe*), and a bottom-fermentation brown beer, known as Donkle Beer.

Founded in 1871 and properly established in 1890, the Diekirch brewery, located in the town of that name, has managed to maintain its independence by concentrating its efforts on exports (to Belgium and France in particular). Diekirch produces nothing but bottom-fermentation beers, using a water source of the highest quality. Its range includes Premium (ABV 4.8 percent), a pilsner in the German tradition; Exclusive (ABV 5.2 percent), which has a slightly malty flavour; and Grande-Réserve (ABV 6.9 percent), an amber-coloured beer. In 1992, Diekirch completed a major modernisation programme, equipping the brewery to compete on equal terms in the European Single Market.

LAMBIC AND GUEUZE BEERS

Epitome of Belgian – or more exactly Brussels – tradition and originality, lambic is a noble beer of ancient pedigree. The method of spontaneous fermentation, which gives it its unique character, is found nowhere else in the world.

Lambic is brewed from malted barley and wheat (35 percent) and flavoured with hops. In making other beers, the brewer tries to keep the hops as fresh as possible, but in the case of lambic the hops are aged to reduce their bitterness.

Instead of adding yeasts to the wort, the lambic brewer simply leaves the liquid

exposed to the air in huge tanks, with all the windows open (lambic is brewed only in winter). Fermentation is therefore caused by the wild yeasts that occur naturally in the Senne valley, South of Brussels, also known as the Pajottenland. This is the only area where lambic is produced. The fermentation process is allowed to continue for months, or even years, in 250-litre barrels or big, 650-litre tuns.

Then, and only then, does the brewer proceed to combine different brews, rather as is done with champagne. Faro, formerly made by blending new and older lambics, is a sweetened version,

now obtained by adding sugar candy to reduce the tartness of the original brew. Gueuze – a word derived from *gueux*, or beggar – is a blend of lambics of different ages, bottled with a champagne-type cork to undergo a second fermentation. It ages well. Another derivation is Kriek, whose recipe includes the rather acid Schaerbeek cherry: 50 kilos are added to every 250 litres of lambic, and left to marinate for between four and eight months. Frambozen is made in the same way, but with raspberries.

An integral part of Brussels culture and tradition, lambics and gueuzes – whose slightly acid taste at first takes the drinker

by surprise – were often blended by café proprietors themselves. They would buy their lambics from the Senne valley brewers, then make beers to their own recipes.

Despite the protection afforded by several royal decrees in recent years, the gueuze generally on sale is sadly often not the authentic Brussels product. Given its popularity, some less scrupulous brewers have tried to speed up the long and difficult production process by blending lambics with other slightly acid beers – beers that bear no relation to lambics. Accusations and controversies to this effect frequently break out in Belgian brewing circles, but for the time being the consumer has no guarantee that he is drinking a genuine gueuze rather than an inferior commercial blend. What is certain is that the large production volumes declared by some brewers are not matched by their capacity to mature the product in suitable storage vessels.

The craze for fruit-flavoured gueuze beers has also given rise to unacceptable practices: syrups and fruit extracts are being used instead of genuine fresh fruit, and there has been a rash of new varieties based on peaches, blackcurrants, plums, and even bananas!

As most of the bottled gueuze beers on the market are at best pale imitations, one must go to some of the old Brussels *bistrots* to savour the real thing. Some of the authentic ones are Cantillon (whose brewer has created a remarkable little museum devoted to gueuze), Girardin, Boon, Timmermans and Eylenbosch. They should be drunk in true Brussels

fashion, with rounds of bread spread with cream cheese and a dish of black radishes.

Over the years, the world of lambic and gueuze has generated a number of colourful personalities, whose

enthusiasm for the product is well described by Raymond Buren in his book *Gueuze, faro et kriek* (published by Glénat). One such was an alderman of Brussels, M. Coelst, chemist and chairman of the Temperance League, who invented a health cure based on gueuze and kriek – believe it or not in the darkest years of the Second World War.

M. Plevoets, another ardent believer in the merits of gueuze, in 1990 wrote to the Confederation of Belgian Brewers in this vein: 'Containing only a minimum of sugar – roughly a quarter of the amount found in other beers – gueuze is a quality product and in no way fattening. At the same time, it is more nutritious,

containing twice the amount of protein and four times the amount of amino-acids. This makes it a high-energy food, and probably explains its medicinal value.'

Yet another passionate 'gueuzier' is Henri Vandervelden. Now over sixty, proud and independent, he cannot bring himself to belong to the Brewers' Confederation. He produces just one gueuze – Oud Beersel – and one kriek – Sherry Poesy – with the greatest respect for the centuries-old tradition. On his property at Beersel,

SUDDEN DEATH AT THE MORT SUBITE

This striking brand name does not refer to the hazards of drinking the gueuze concerned, but derives from a game of dice – *zanzi* – that was played at a Brussels café, then known as the *Cour Royale*, in the early years of the century. The café was frequented by employees of the neighbouring Banque de Belgique and by journalists, who would often spend their time gambling. On occasions when their professional duties forced them to break off the game they were playing, they would each finish with a single throw: hence the expression 'mort subite', or sudden death, which was always accompanied by a great downing of gueuze. Théophile Vossen, the astute proprietor of the café, renamed his establishment accordingly. Forced to move in 1926 to rue de la Montagne-aux-Herbes, the café (which is still well worth a visit) retained this name, with a sense of humour quite typical of Brussels: its neighbour at the time was an undertaker!

to the south of Brussels (virtually the only place you can get to taste his products), he has organised a small museum of ancient tools and artefacts from times past.

Another fierce defender of the tradition, Jean-Pierre Van Roy, a teacher by profession, fell in love with gueuze over twenty years ago. His passion began when he met his future wife, the daughter of a brewer located in rue Gueude, right in the heart of Brussels. He eventually took over the brewery and now produces the Cantillon range, one of the most genuine in the region. To educate the public, he has started a gueuze museum on his premises (open every Saturday from October to May and on weekdays by appointment). He now receives 20,000 visitors annually, and twice a year brews his beer in public. Nicknamed the 'David of gueuze' (who are the Goliaths?, one might well ask), Jean-Pierre Van Roy produces a gueuze made entirely from lambic beers, a krieklambic based on real cherries, a frambozen named Rosé de Gambrinus and a faro. He has also reinstated an ancient type of gueuze in which he marinates muscat grapes: a reconciliation between beer and wine. You really must taste his Brabantiae, a matured gueuze, first produced in 1991 to mark the sixtieth birthday of King Baudouin.

GERMANY

Because it is home to 40 percent of the world's brewers and has for many years held the record for consumption per head (currently 140 litres a year), Germany has a unique place as both producer and consumer of beer. Amid the welter of facts and figures, it is important to realise how central a role beer plays in daily life, and has done for centuries. Every sizeable town, and many a village, has its own brewery, as much a part of the scenery as church or *Sparkasse* (savings bank). Undisputed queen of every festival (and despite their reputation for grim discipline, the Germans are a fun-loving race), beer is an ever-present companion. Less imaginative than the Belgians but more willing to accept change than the British, German brewers are faithful first and foremost to their regional style of beer. In a given region you will find only minor differences between one brewery and another, whereas the differences between regions – say between Hamburg and Cologne – can be quite striking. Long spared the takeovers and mergers that have changed the face of the brewing industry in other countries, post-reunification Germany is now beginning to feel the harsh wind of economic necessity. But the signs are that the average German would still prefer to sup his local brew rather than a national or international brand.

The Mass, *or litre mug, emblematic of Munich's* Oktoberfest.

PILSNERS OF THE NORTH

Invented a hundred and fifty years ago by brewers in the Czech town of Plzen (Pilsen in German), beers of the pilsner type undoubtedly have the widest distribution throughout Germany. Given their quality and faithfulness to the original, it would be unfair to refer to them as lagers, the term commonly used to describe the rank and file of blond, bottom-fermentation beers.

Mainstay of most German brewers, pilsner beers are an essential ingredient in daily living. Of relatively low density, they are suitable for drinking both in and outside the home. Drawing a glass of this beer is a real art, and there are specialised bodies at local and regional level to check the quality of the product as served in bars and cafés. Pasteurised only in exceptional cases, pilsner beer is highly digestible and easily eliminated from the system.

Unlike the Belgians and Alsatians, who use a coupe-mousse to draw a glass of beer without froth, German barmen are

more generous in their way of serving, drawing several times on the pump to present a brimming glass of beer – usually of tall format – with a head several centimetres thick. By the same token, their beer is packaged in 50-centilitre bottles, a measure that has virtually disappeared elsewhere.

The further north you go, the more pilsner beer dominates. Hamburg is one of its strongholds: here the Czech original collected its first international award way back in 1863! And Hamburg brewers were among the first in Germany to use hops on a large scale.

Not far from Hamburg, Jever in Friesland is home to one of the country's most highly hopped pilsners, registering 42 units of bitterness, and similar beers are brewed in the great port itself. The biggest brewer is undoubtedly Holsten, producer of Diät-Pils, followed by Moravia (in the neighbouring town of Lüneburg) and Dressler.

Another big Hamburg brewer is Bavaria St-Pauli. The name is deceptive – there is nothing Bavarian about it – and to add to the confusion, Hamburg's sister city of Bremen has a brewery called the St-Pauli Girl. Bremen also boasts the oldest brewers' corporation in the world, founded in 1489, and there are close ties between the various brewers, some even sharing facilities. Beck's is the best-known beer and is widely exported (locally, it is sold as Haake-Beck), together with the Hemelinger and Remmer brands. The town is also renowned for its *Weissebier*, wheat-based beers similar to those produced in Berlin.

Unlike Bavaria, the north and northwest

MADE IN GERMANY

German brewers may be renowned for their seriousness and loyalty to regional traditions, but they are also capable of exercising their imaginations. Proof of the fact are these two German creations, distributed in France by *les Artisans de la bière: la Cervoise des Ancêtres* – as drunk by Asterix and Co.! – comes in a stoneware bottle (which you can take home with you), while *la Bière des Aviateurs* (Pilot's beer) is sold in a superb metal bottle bearing portraits of Lindbergh and other pioneers of flight. Germany also produces beer in glass bottles in the shape of a monk or bishop. They sell like hot cakes, and the contents go down well, too!

of Germany have seen the development of many 'single-product' breweries, producing enormous volumes of a single beer in highly controlled conditions. Warsteiner is the biggest, with an output of almost five million hectolitres. Others major brewers who have attempted the difficult task of capturing a national market are König, Bitburger (nearer to the Saarland), Karlsberg (nothing to do with the celebrated Danish firm; its export beers in any case bear the name

Karlsbrau), and Krombacher.

Although in such places as Hannover, Brunswick, Münster or the Hanseatic towns drinkers still show a preference for locally-brewed beers, mergers are tending to take place at regional level. These new groupings are, however, chiefly financial

in character, with no intention of reducing the number of distinct brands. For instance, there are financial ties between the brewers of Dortmund, Frankfurt and Berlin, or again between brewing interests in Mannheim, Nuremberg and other towns.

Münster, by the way, still has a unique style of beer brewed from wheat, produced by the ancient firm of Pinkus Muller.

In northern Germany, though, regional differences are of little significance and there is less variety of styles than in the south. Specialists may talk till the cows come home of shades of hoppiness, density or dryness between the beers of one town and another, but in reality one German pilsner is very much like the next. The best policy is to do as the Germans do: wherever you are, drink the local beer. You are unlikely to be disappointed.

THE RHINELAND

The major cities of the Rhineland have each maintained their own style of beer. The further south one travels towards Switzerland, the greater the part played by small local breweries.

Dortmund, in the Ruhr, is the brewing capital of Germany's industrial heartland. Although it ranks high in terms of production, its beers are not so well known as they deserve. True, its premier beer has not a very inspiring title: DAB, the initials standing for Dortmunder Actien Bräuerei, Dortmund Breweries plc! Another major company with a similarly unpromising name – DUB – came into being a century ago when a number of independent brewers merged.

These and the town's other important breweries – Kronen, Thier and Hansa – have one thing in common: the Dortmunder Export style. A bottom-fermentation beer, it has more body than a traditional pilsner but is less sweet than a Bavarian brew. A subtle palate is required to distinguish between the thirty or so different varieties of this basic style, with several of the town's breweries offering a range of related products.

Though located at the junction of Rhine and Ruhr, the König brewery at Duisburg is typical of the single-product enterprise we encountered in the north of Germany. Over one hundred and thirty years old and managed by the same family for five generations, König stakes all on its highly-hopped, extremely bitter beer, relying on the very latest brewing technology to ensure a quality product. The brewer's only concession to modern-day fashions is an alcohol-free beer, Kelt, introduced onto the market a few years back. In the case of König, a combination of tradition and clever marketing has paid dividends:

faithfulness to a single, high-quality product is today enabling König to approach both German and foreign markets with a solidly established brand. Düsseldorf, the financial capital of the Ruhr, is also the home of *altbier*, an appropriate name for the 'old' beers that

did not succumb when the fashion for bottom fermentation hit Germany in the last century. It is impossible to say why this modern city should have remained a bastion of the older style of beer – a style still very much alive and kicking in Belgium and the UK. A number of Düsseldorf micro-breweries have adopted *altbier* as their speciality. They also offer favoured customers occasional brews: denser, dry-hopped beers which last only a day or two. You may have the good fortune to run one of them to earth at *Zum Uerige*, the most famous of these

establishments.

Some of the best-known *altbiers* are the amber-coloured Schlösser Alt and the slightly sweeter Gatzweilers, both produced in Düsseldorf itself, and the celebrated Hannen Alt, brewed in Mönchengladbach. Beers of this kind have become extremely popular, for instance the Diebels brewery at Issum produced over 1.5 million hectolitres of its fine Alt in 1992, an increase of 50 percent in the last ten years.

As compared with British ales or Belgian abbey beers, German *altbier* is more highly hopped and clean flavoured, but lower in fruitiness or acidity. Amber is the

---

BEER AND SCHNAPPS

Drinking beer together with schnapps – a spirit generally distilled from maize – is still a current practice in Germany. In some regions, the two are downed in one go. The drinker holds two small (5 centilitre) glasses in his hand, one full of beer, the other of schnapps. As he tips them back together, the schnapps runs first into the beer then on into the awaiting mouth. As spectacular as it is hazardous, this procedure is only learned by practice!

---

usual colour. Beers of this type are also found in some other north German towns, notably Münster, Essen and Hannover (which produces the superb, copper-coloured Broyhan Alt).

A little further south, Cologne also boasts a style of beer all its own: Kölsch, still produced by a dozen or so breweries in the city itself and a similar number in the

surrounding area – a record in itself. The name is assiduously protected and may not be encroached on by inferior products.

Kölsch is one of the few top-fermentation beers still brewed in Germany, but very different from its British and Belgian

GERMANY

counterparts: pale with a touch of gold, its character lies not so much in its strength or bitterness as in its subtle aroma, which is strangely reminiscent of the local white wines. It owes its uniqueness to the use of soft water, conditioning in a cool environment (unusual for a top-fermentation beer) and its sustained, but not excessive, bitterness.

Ideal as an aperitif, Kölsch offers a subtle hint of herbs or cereals, as if wheat had been added, but it is in fact brewed from pure barley malt. A number of interesting versions are sold by local micro-breweries, and though this type of beer is best drunk on the spot, Cologne's largest brewer, Küppers, markets an excellent Kölsch throughout Germany and abroad.

Continuing our journey up the Rhine, we continue to find pilsners of high quality: Henninger of Frankfurt, Eichbaum of Mannheim or Dinkelacker of Stuttgart,

whose CD-Pils has nothing to do with the ubiquitous Compact-Disc but owes its name to Carl Dinkelacker, the company's founder. Not all breweries market their products under a specific brand name, for instance Riegel, opposite the French town of Colmar in the Baden Württemberg region, or Braunfels, in Hessen, are identified simply by the name of their town of origin.

The Binding brewery in Frankfurt is, in volume terms, the biggest in all Germany, producing a complete range of beers which includes its famous Export Privat. It is also unique in brewing a beer exclusively for the American market, under the name of Steinhauser.

Mainz, near Frankfurt, was the home of Arnold Busch, who in the last century left Germany for the United States to found what is now the biggest brewery in the world. At Limburg, in the same region, there is still a Busch family involved in brewing, but its products have little in common with those of the American colossus.

In Mannheim, Eichbaum is justly proud of its three-hundred-year tradition, tracing its origins to 1697, when a certain Jean de Chaîne founded a brewery known as *Zum Aichbaum*. The town still supported forty or so breweries at the beginning of the nineteenth century, but today Eichbaum, the oldest, is the only one still in operation – proof of prodigious vitality. Its range includes no less than three *Weizenbier*, a Doppel Bock (Apostulator) and, expressing a commendable concern for tradition, the lighter Ureich pilsner (the prefix 'ur' signifies 'original', therefore 'Ureich' means 'original oak'). To get this point across, the company features the

ancient Germans and their drinking horns in its advertising campaigns. In association with other German brewers (notably Henninger, the number two in Frankfurt), Eichbaum now produces over a million hectolitres of beer a year.

Coming at length to the Black Forest, we find a number of small breweries nestling picturesquely in the attractive hollows and valleys of the region. Ketterer and Hirsch are typical examples. Slightly less bitter than their northern counterparts, their pilsner beers are nevertheless quite

equal to quenching the thirst of energetic ramblers and nature lovers.

In general, the breweries in this region are more inclined to diversify production than their big, single-product rivals to the north. The standard pilsner is often flanked by a less heavy variety, known as Leicht. This is somewhat surprising when one considers that even the standard version has a fairly low alcohol content, between 4.5 and 5 percent ABV at most. Alcohol-free beers are also gaining ground, as is *Weizenbier*, produced in imitation of its Bavarian original.

The only exception to the trend towards diversification is the aristocratic Fürstenberg brewery, at Donauess-chingen, famous for its pilsner beer and for an astonishing collection of paintings housed in the adjacent castle.

Sold almost exclusively in their home town and the immediately surrounding area, these pilsners (sometimes called Hellbier [=light/bright/pale beer]) are not normally intended to travel and are therefore rarely pasteurised, which gives them a remarkable freshness and vivacity. They tend to be drunk very young.

Foreign beer enthusiasts are unlikely to encounter them beyond the confines of Germany. One should in any case be wary of 'Export' versions of certain German beers, because the pasteurisation process they generally undergo robs them of their aromatic qualities. The fact remains that German pilsners, because of the careful attention paid to the way they are hopped, still have a distinctive bitterness, a characteristic nowadays in abeyance in other parts of Europe.

FRANCONIA

Franconia (Franken in German) is the northeastern part of Bavaria. There would be no reason for treating this area separately from Germany's biggest province but for the fact that its brewing industry is of special interest.

First of all, it has even more breweries to the square kilometres than Bavaria itself, which is no mean record: every town, almost every large village, has a brewery to its name. Secondly, in addition to the more common pilsners, Franconia is home to some quite unique beers.

Let us begin with one of the world's strongest beers, EKU 28 (13.5 percent ABV), just beaten by the Swiss Samichlaus, but with only two or three decimal points in it. The German beer is, however, slightly denser, and in any case results tend to vary from one analysis to another. Brewed at Kulmbach, EKU is amber-coloured rather than dark. The three letters stand for the name of the brewery: Erste (meaning first), Kulmbach and Union (recording the fact that two breweries united a century or so ago). EKU 28 has a gestation period of nine months, but the brewery also numbers some quicker-maturing beers in its range.

Franconia is renowned for its dark lagers, produced in such historic centres as Amberg, Nuremberg, Bamberg (home to ten or so thriving breweries), Bayreuth, Cobourg and many others. The region

even has municipal breweries where the locals can go to brew their own beer!

One of Franconia's most original products is undoubtedly the *Rauchbier*, or smoked beer, brewed in Bamberg. During kilning, the malt is heated over smoking beechwood fires, rather as the Scots use

THE MYSTERY OF 'KRÄUSENING'

Though sometimes practised in other parts of Germany, the technique of 'kräusening' is a speciality of Franconia. It consists in adding a small quantity of green beer to the fermenting wort, which gives a boost to the fermentation process and increases the carbon dioxide content of the finished product. Kräusen beers are generally not filtered and, when poured, develop a generous head.

peat fires in producing malt whisky.

This process gives the beer an amazing smoky tang, not always obvious at the first sip, but whose flavour lingers on the palate. A brewer at Cham, near Regensburg, goes even further, maturing his beer on a bed of beech chippings to give an even stronger flavour.

Though similar in taste, the Steinbier (stone beer) produced at Rauchenfels near Cobourg is produced by a quite different method, dating from times when mash tuns could not be heated directly. The brewer heats stones over a beech fire to temperatures in excess of 1,000 °C, then tips them into the vessel containing the wort, which rapidly brings it to the boil. The stones are left in the beer during maturation, the caramelised sugars on their surfaces causing a secondary fermentation. The end result is a strong, full-bodied, smoky-flavoured beer.

Although they are not its exclusive preserve, Franconia also specialises in *Eisbock* beers, strong brews obtained by the process of freezing. Since alcohol has a lower freezing point than water, it is possible to increase the alcohol content of a beer by freezing it. The town of Kulmbach is a great centre of this activity. Finally, Franconia is unique in still having a number of breweries operated by steam

power. The Maisel brewery at Bayreuth even produces a top-fermentation Dampfbier (steam beer). The only other country still using such antiquated methods is Belgium.

Founded just over a century ago by two brothers, Hans and Eberhardt, the Maisel brewery faithfully reflects the whole gamut of beers brewed in Franconia. Maisel produce three wheat beers, all by top fermentation: the fresh-tasting Hefe Weissbier; Weizen Kristallklar, clear and so sparkling you could mistake it for champagne; and the stronger Weizen Bock, which is drunk mainly in winter.

The range also includes a diet beer, a conventional pilsner, a stronger beer – Original 1887 – and an alcohol-free product: something to satisfy every taste.

BERLIN

Without wanting to offend the worthy merchants of Rheims and Epernay, Germany has its own champagne, produced in Berlin. Such at least is the burden of an anecdote dating from the arrival of Napoleon's troops in the Prussian capital: tasting *Weissbier* for the first time, they immediately dubbed it 'northern champagne'.

Light and refreshing, Berlin's white beer is a top-fermentation product using between 25 and 50 percent of malted wheat in the brewing process. It differs from its Munich counterparts in having a very low alcohol content, not more than 3 percent ABV; nor are spices added to it, as in Belgium. A table beer if ever there was one, it is acidic in taste rather than bitter, hops being used in minimal quantities and only for the sake of their keeping properties.

This is not surprising, given that the yeast involved is the result of symbiosis between a top-fermentation strain and a bacillus found in milk, isolated at the beginning of the century by Prof. Delbrück of the Institute of Brewing in Berlin. Normally, brewers would avoid this bacillus like the plague, but those of Berlin have learnt to tame it, thereby giving a unique character to their beer.

Because it is not heavily filtered, Berlin white beer is slightly cloudy and retains sufficient of its yeasts to continue fermenting in the bottle. The result is a beverage which sparkles agreeably when poured into the glass.

Berliners prefer to drink it in wide, goblet-shaped glasses, sometimes adding fruit flavourings – particularly raspberry or wild strawberry – to reduce its natural acidity. A truly popular drink, it is available only in summer – just the thing to drink *unter den Linden* during a heatwave.

The division of Berlin did not affect people's liking for Weissebier, which continued to be drunk on both sides of the wall. In the West, it was brewed by Berliner Kindl or Schultheiss (now a member of the Dortmunder Union group); in the East, by the Sailerbräu or Berliner Weisse breweries.

As in the rest of the former East Germany, reunification has led to changes in the organisation of the city's brewing industry. Mergers, take-overs, absorptions: the scramble began the moment the wall was down, especially since brewers in the West, their markets already at saturation point, were looking for profitable new sales outlets.

Political differences had in any case hardly any bearing on people's drinking habits. East Germans had always drunk as much beer as their brothers and sisters in the West, and there was little difference in the types of beer they favoured. East German breweries, on the other hand, had not benefited from the modern technology available elsewhere. Consequently, they were less productive – and considerably less competitive in the reunified market.

Since 1989, the brewing industry has undergone rapid change, with the West Germans generally keeping the whip hand. It is not so much the breweries that have been affected as the distribution networks they controlled, with the new owners anxious to sell their own products as widely as possible. A further factor is that brewers in the West have demanded that the purity law be strictly applied in the East, which was not the case in the past.

The results have been entirely predictable. Brau und Brunnen, one of the leading German groups, has signed cooperation

agreements with Berlin's Schultheiss, Kindl and Engelhardt breweries, with the barely concealed intention of becoming the majority shareholder. Another major company, the Binding group of Frankfurt, has bought a stake in the Radeberg and Krostitzer breweries in Saxony (Radeberg was a market leader in the former GDR), in the Potsdamer Brauerei, and in the Burgerbrau brewery in East Berlin. In buying out the Leipzig brewery, Paulaner of Munich made no secret of the fact that it was the associated network of sixty wholesale outlets it really wanted to acquire.

The case of Freiberger is revealing in this respect: the firm produced 100,000 hectolitres in 1989; 50,000 in 1990; then 400,000 in 1991, once its purchase by the Eichbaum brewery of Mannheim began to bear fruit. Modernised and animated by a

new way of thinking, the breweries of the former GDR have become powerful rivals to their counterparts in the West. The fact is that they are better placed to wage a price war, having continued to pay lower salaries to their workers. Even so, according to a study carried out by the German Institute of Commerce, of the one hundred and fifty breweries formerly operating in East Germany, 50 percent are likely to disappear in the near future – too antiquated for successful modernisation.

Not being highly regarded, East German beers at first suffered from the influx of prestigious beers from the West, whether German or not. Latterly, it would seem that tradition has reasserted itself, with East Germans going back to their local brews, especially since they continue to be cheaper.

After the wave of mergers, acquisitions and closures, what will be the fate of beers from Leipzig or East Berlin? In the opinion those familiar with East German beers prior to reunification, there were some interesting specialities, particularly some of the brown beers. We shall have to wait a while for the situation to clarify. Only then will it be possible to take stock of the brewing industry and its products in the eastern part of Germany.

BEER FESTIVALS

The importance of beer in German culture is best illustrated by the annual beer festivals, attended by thousands, who sit at long tables supping huge mugs of beer to the sonorous strains of a brass band. Every beer lover should savour the experience at least once.

The oldest and most famous is undoubtedly the Oktoberfest, a two-week celebration held every autumn in Munich in a large meadow adjacent to the city centre. In 1810, the prince of Bavaria wanted to marry a Prussian princess, but the match was unpopular and, to placate his subjects, he felt obliged to lay on a grandiose festival. Ever since, the festival has been celebrated annually, increasing in importance as time has gone by.

Today, the Oktoberfest attracts over 7 million participants. In the midst of a

gigantic funfair (with certain entertainments well worth visiting for their own sake), each of the Munich breweries erects its own temporary pavilion, which may comfortably seat 7,000 people. At peak times, as many again will be standing in the aisles. In the centre is a raised platform for the traditional brass band. In the four corners and serving areas, bevies of waiters and

The Oktoberfest *is the greatest beer festival in the world. Only a stone's throw from Munich's cathedral, it also offers all the fun of the fair. Some of the waitresses can carry eight to ten litre mugs at a time!*

waitresses are to be seen bustling to and fro with fistfuls of the obligatory litre mugs, known as *Mass*, and plates of chicken and sausages, traditional accompaniment to the beer. The Marzenbier drunk at the Oktoberfest is delivered to the site in 1,000-litre tankers. The ritual is always the same. The first drinkers take their places around midday and a festival atmosphere is quickly created: orders are placed and beer is drunk; the band plays and at regular intervals has everyone on their feet for interminable toasts. Drinkers withdraw to the toilettes, then come back and begin again! This continues until a quarter to eleven exactly, when, as if by magic, the band packs up, the lights go out, and the crowd files out into the night. In ten minutes, it is all over. The peace and quiet in the pavilions is as startling as the thunderous noise and celebrations that prevailed only minutes earlier. And tomorrow it will all begin again .... In all, 60,000 hectolitres of beer, 700,000 chickens and 500,000 sausages will be consumed in the course of the Oktoberfest.

Just as unchanging and unchangeable is the traditional procession. It lasts two hours, punctuated at intervals by the drays of the Munich brewers, drawn by six, in some cases eight, horses. Many are still in regular service, particularly for deliveries within the city limits.

Other major beer festivals are held at Hannover, in the north, and in other German cities, not forgetting the famous Rhineland carnivals. But there is also a whole host of local festivals, especially in the summer time, where beer reigns supreme, often brewed specially for the occasion.

or 'to preserve'. Debased as this term may now be in many parts of the world, its original meaning is still valid here.

In Bavaria, the cold-conditioning process was first applied to relatively dark-coloured beers, known as *Dunkel*, with a high malt content and only a hint of hops. Of only average strength, 'Munich' beers

BAVARIA

Without Munich, and Bavaria, the beer-drinking world would be a poorer place. Besides being the biggest beer drinkers in the world (240 litres per adult per annum), the Bavarians have invented a wide range of different beers. These are best sampled in Munich's *Bierhalle*, vast beer halls holding several thousand people at a time. The biggest, the Mäthaser, which belongs to the Löwenbräu brewery, has seating for 5,000, in fifteen or so large rooms. In summer, the local beer gardens, in both town and country, are among the most pleasant places in the world to enjoy a leisurely mug of foaming beer.

Beer has undoubtedly been brewed in Bavaria from time immemorial, but this part of Germany has also played a central role in the modern history of brewing, perfecting the techniques of bottom fermentation and cold conditioning. Though it was discovered as far back as the 15th century – as proved by municipal records dating from 1429 – the process was not really developed until the last century, and it is the Czechs of Plzen who must take the credit for the first bottom-fermentation beers.

The contribution of the Munich brewers, particularly Gabriel Sedlmayr, was in mastering the conditioning process in cold-store conditions, which gave rise to the term 'lager', meaning simply 'to keep'

quickly won favour beyond the borders of Bavaria and were taken up by breweries all round the world. Outside its country of origin, the term Munich beer is nowadays used to describe a lager-type beer of brown coloration.

The end of the last century saw the development of a second standard style of lager: Münchner Hell (or Munich light) – golden coloured, almost blond, less bitter than a pilsner, with a special variant for export purposes.

Another famous Munich brew is *Märzenbier*: the beer brewed in March, kept throughout the summer and served in October at the great beer festival. Malty in flavour, amber coloured, translucent and rather strong, these beers are related to those of Vienna and have nothing in common with the *bières de Mars* nowadays served in France on the first hot summer days.

Although it has its origins elsewhere, Bock beer has also found its fullest

expression in Munich (you will not win many friends if you mention that it was first brewed at Einbeck in Lower Saxony). A Bock is a stronger-than-average beer, generally amber coloured (though pale versions also exist) and traditionally drunk in spring (which is why it is sometimes referred to as Maibock). Even

stronger are Double Bock beers (7 percent ABV or more), which were popularised by Munich's biggest brewery, the Paulaner. The monks of St Paul's, who owned the brewery in the 17th century, brewed this nourishing beer during the Lenten fast and gave it the name of Salvator, or saviour. The ceremony of broaching the first barrel of Salvator is performed each year in the run-up to Easter, in the presence of the mayor of Munich and the Bavarian prime minister, and draws a crowd of several thousand. The style was imitated by other Bavarian breweries, who also chose names for their

Double Bocks ending in -ator. There are more than a hundred of them in the regions of Bavaria and Baden-Württemberg: Animator, Triumphator, Optimator, Celebrator, Buronator, Rigolator, and so on. There are nevertheless a number of excellent Double Bocks which do not follow this convention, for instance Quirinus, from Upper Bavaria; Andechs, a beer with a wine-like flavour, from the ancient monastery of that name; or Schäff, a strong beer brewed at Treuchlingen, ABV 10 percent.

We have still not exhausted the list of Munich beers: besides the alcohol-free and low-alcohol beers that every German brewer is nowadays expected to supply, we must take into account the *Weizenbier* style, now rapidly gaining favour. Closely related to the 'white' beers of Belgium and the *Weisse* brewed in Berlin, Munich's *Weizenbier* originates from the Hofbräuhaus, formerly the brewery of the Bavarian court, now owned by the regional government. A top-fermentation

THE SEDLMAYR DYNASTY

Many Munich and Bavarian breweries can trace their roots back several centuries (the oldest claims to have been founded in 1040), with the same family in control over many generations. Spaten is typical in this respect: established in the 14th century, it derives its emblem and name (meaning shovel – the tool used in spreading the malting barley) from its founder, a certain Spaeth. The strongest influence on its development has been the Sedlmayr family, which took over the brewery at the beginning of the 19th century and is still in control today. In conjunction with the great Austrian brewer Anton Dreher, Gabriel Sedlmayr the Younger created the Munich-style lager and promoted the development of the first refrigerator, an invention which has freed brewers the world over from seasonal constraints. On this account, Sedlmayr has some claim to be considered the father of bottom-fermentation beers.

beer based on wheat (at least 50 percent and often more), *Weizenbier* is brewed using a special strain of yeast, which gives the beer a slightly acid, fruity flavour - excellent as a thirst-quencher. It has a cloudy appearance, due to yeast suspended in the liquid. According to Michael Jackson, 'the fashion for *Weizenbier*, in places as far apart as Munich and Milwaukee, is a sure sign of the renewed interest in beer'.

Weizenbier is, as the name suggests, generally whitish in colour, but there are also darker versions, such as the excellent Ur-Weizen produced by the Ayinger brewery. Another variant of these wheat-based beers is the *Weizenbock* type, for instance the Schneider-brewed Aventinus, which has a higher alcohol content. This is an amazing combination, bringing together a full-bodied malt flavour and the aromatic and slightly acid character of wheat.

Though usually served on draught, *Weizenbier* can also be enjoyed in bottled form, in which case they are further improved by a secondary fermentation. Signal examples are the heady Alte Weisse from Augsburg or, from Nuremberg, the Tucher Hefe Weizen, which has a spicy, aromatic nose.

All these Munich styles vary considerably from brewer to brewer, which ensures an ever-changing range of flavours to enjoy throughout the year. The beer-drinker is spoilt for choice, each brewer having his own interpretation of what a Bock or Weizen should be. Bavaria's brewers are many in number and vital to the local economy. Munich itself is famous for its 'six sisters': Paulaner, Spaten, Löwenbräu,

Augustiner, Hacker-Pschorr and the Hofbräuhaus. With traditions going back several centuries, all still have premises within the city limits and, in their respective *Bierhalle*, offer a dozen or so different beers, depending on the time of year.

Hacker-Pschorr has particularly close links with the city and its history, due largely to the strong personality of Joseph Pschorr, who owned the brewery for much of the 19th century. The emblem of the Hacker brewery, founded in the 15th, was two crossed carpenters' axes – the workmen employed in enlarging the city having been its first customers. When he married Thérèse Hacker in 1793, Joseph Pschorr took over the business and set

about developing it, still finding time and energy to acquire a second brewery in 1820. Such is his reputation that he is the only brewer to be commemorated on the site of the gigantic Oktoberfest, where his bust takes its place beside the statue representing Bavaria. On his death, each of his two sons inherited a brewery. These went their separate ways until 1972, when

THE PURITY EDICT OF 1516

In 1516, William IV, Elector of Bavaria, promulgated an edict stating that 'only malt, barley, hops and water, and no other substance' might be used in brewing beverages claiming the name of beer. The purpose of this law was to safeguard the quality of beer in the face of a proliferation of secular brewers, some of whom were using bizarre ingredients in their mash tubs. During this period, the authorities in other countries were also moved to take similar measures: in Artois, in 1550, a regulation was passed forbidding brewers to use lime or soap during the brewing process. It is interesting that the 1516 text makes no mention of yeast as an authorised ingredient: in those days, brewers were quite ignorant of its existence, relying instead on spontaneous fermentation. The law was given a new lease of life in 1976, when, to protect their own products, German brewers resorted to it to halt imports of foreign beers, notably from Alsace. In 1987, without calling the 1516 edict into question, the European Court of Justice ruled that Germany should not use the edict again for this purpose.

they finally merged. In 1980 they became part of the Paulaner group, but still enjoy autonomy in commercial and technical matters.

Perfect illustration of the hold beer has over Munich, prince Luitpold of Bavaria, a descendant of the former kings, himself brews beer in his castle at Kaltenberg, near Munich. His brewery is renowned for its dark lager, König Ludwig Dunkel.

Note that Paulaner has also opened a micro-brewery on Munich's Kapuzinerplatz, an establishment resplendent in copper, wood-carving and stained glass, marble and ceramics.

Even a giant may take an interest in smaller-scale activities, though there is nothing inferior about the beer, which is excellent.

Ideally, all the beers we have mentioned need to be drunk *in situ*: their export versions are generally disappointing, having been pasteurised to enable them to travel. In choosing from the wide range

on offer, it is best to follow the example of the Bavarians themselves. They know which beer is most appropriate to the season and time of day!

Other Bavarian breweries need feel no sense of inferiority in relation to their 'big sisters' in the capital. There are still over eight hundred of them, some producing no more than one or two thousand hectolitres a year. Many are quite content to rule the roost in their own town or village, but others have begun to make a name for themselves further afield. One example is the Ayinger brewery, located in a small village outside Munich, which markets one of the largest ranges of Bavarian beers. Its products include Jahrhundert, a perfect example of the Munich export style; a Double Bock named Fortunator; a Maibock; and, last but not least, Ur-Weizen, a darkish wheat beer, unfiltered and highly aromatic. These can all be enjoyed in the heart of Munich, at the Platzl brasserie, where there are also regular performances by traditional song-and-dance troupes.

Schneider, whose brewery is now located outside the city, still has one of the finest beer-drinking establishments in Munich, on the Tal Strasse. Erdinger specialises in *Weissbier*: Kristallklar, a classic, clear beer, with no trace of yeast; and Pikantus, a smooth, bottle-conditioned brown.

Fifteen or twenty miles from Munich, Weihenstephan can claim to be the oldest working brewery in the world, the monks having begun brewing there in 1040. It passed into lay hands during the 19th century and now belongs to the Bavarian State. Though one may still find vestiges of the Middle Ages, the installations have been modernised time and again, and the present-day beers (in particular some distinguished whites) are certainly not mashed in the original tubs. This brewery also houses one of Bavaria's schools of brewing, a faculty of the University of Munich.

Though each beer is to be drunk in due season, it is rarely drunk on its own. Bavaria has a whole range of foods for eating with beer, first and foremost the ubiquitous sausage, which must rival beer itself in the number of traditional varieties produced. *Weisswurst*, a white sausage made from veal, is especially delicious. And be sure to try a black radish or two.

SWITZERLAND

At first sight, the Swiss brewing industry presents a contradiction: as well as brewing the strongest beer in the world – Hürlimann's Samichlaus – it was one of the first to produce alcohol-free beers! The contradiction is more apparent than real: both phenomena derive from the same concern for quality that has always characterised brewing in Switzerland.

For many years Swiss beer was produced on a local scale, mediocre in quality and dearer than wine. Not until the last century did it really take off. It is true that the abbey at Sankt Gallen housed a brewing establishment of high repute from as early as the 11th century, but the manufacture of beer was of little significance until the industrial revolution. From 120,000 hectolitres in 1850, production increased to a million hectolitres over the next thirty-five years, and in that time the number of breweries more than tripled.

Neutral but extremely protectionist in matters of trade, the Federal government sought from an early stage to protect the

country from the evils of competition, both internal and external, especially where beer was concerned. The Swiss Brewers' Association was founded in 1877 and, following a 1907 agreement forestalling any price war between brewers 'in the interests of the consumer', in 1935 set up a cartel. This arrangement limited the sale of beer to its canton of origin and effectively prevented foreign brewers from penetrating the Swiss market, unless they were associated with a local firm. A more deliberate case of protectionism would be hard to find in the annals of the brewing industry, as other countries have generally relied on their consumers' preference for national products.

Even so, this system did not prevent a concentration of brewing interests: the number of breweries dropped from one hundred and twenty-six in 1915 to fifty nine in 1970. And by the end of the 1980s only thirty or so remained.

Three groups currently dominate the market: Feldschlösschen, based at Rheinfelden near Basel, which is more or less directly associated with Wartechk of Basel, Gurten of Berne, Valaisanne of Sion, Haldengut of Winterthur and Calanda of Chur; Hürlimann of Zürich, which has links with Löwenbräu (nothing to do with the famous Munich brewery) and brews Carlsberg beers under licence; and Sibra-Holding, a 1970 grouping of five breweries led by Cardinal of Fribourg, which has imposed its brands on Beauregard, Fertig, Weber and Salmenbräu.

In 1991 the Swiss brewing industry

suffered what amounted to an implosion: firstly, the French giant Kronenbourg, which had been nibbling at the Swiss market for many years, managed to sign a partnership agreement with the market leader Feldschlösschen; then, just a few months later, Feldschlösschen joined forces with the Sibra group (Cardinal beers). As a result, the cartel fell to pieces at the end of the year, to the great satisfaction of brewers eager to extend their operations to

the whole national market.

Although there is now an open field for competition, it is unlikely that, initially at least, we shall see any big changes in the range of beers on offer. Swiss drinkers seem to be inherently conservative, even though they are now showing more interest in imported beers.

Bottom-fermentation lager, almost exclusively of the blond type with an ABV rating of between 4.2 and 5.3 percent, is the most popular drink, closely followed by stronger, more highly hopped special brews. The national range also includes an alcohol-free beer (which the Swiss were among the first to produce); a low-alcohol beer; a pure-malt blond; and, in some cases, seasonal beers. In terms of technique, Swiss breweries tend to mature their bottom-fermentation beers for longer periods – from three to six months – which gives them a finer flavour.

The Feldschlösschen brewery lives up to its name (little castle in the country).

The Hürlimann brewery, Zürich, founded in 1865 and extended several times over the years.

Rather than a defensive stronghold, it comes straight out of an operetta, complete with fanciful turrets and battlements. The building, a former chemicals factory, in any case antedates the brewery, which took over the premises in 1874. The name derives from an old German brewery in Brunswick, where the founder, Théophil Roninger, had worked in his youth.

The choice of location, just outside Basel, was determined by the proximity of the Basel-Zürich railway line and has proved to be a judicious one: Feldschlösschen has always taken advantage of the railways to distribute its products. It has also shown considerable talent for absorbing its rivals, with twenty-three takeovers to its credit in the years 1882 to 1930! – and has continued in this vein, finally to become the market leader. The stars of its somewhat predictable range of beers are the dryish special Hopfenperle blond and the related Dunkleperle brown, Fest 1876, and the strong, full-bodied Castello.

There was a Hürlimann brewery in Zürich as early as 1836, but the business was subsequently sold by its founder, Hans Hürlimann. The brewery we see today was founded in 1865 by his son, Albert, who had learned his trade in Bavaria. From that time on, the Hürlimann story has been one of steady growth and expansion.

Having many years' experience of yeasts and the fermentation process, Hürlimann both specialises in alcohol-free beers such as Birell (one of the most widely sold in Switzerland) and produces the strongest beer in the world (see adjacent box). Its very full range includes a classical lager, ABV 4.8 percent (of which there is also a

brown version); Sternbräu, a special beer with a distinctly malty flavour (ABV 5.2 percent); Gold, a premium beer with barely a touch of bitterness (ABV 5.1 percent); Hexenbräu, meaning 'witches' brew', a relatively mild brown; and Dreikonigs, a strong, blond beer, hoppy in

SAMICHLAUS, THE STRONGEST BEER IN THE WORLD

In 1982, Hürlimann found its way into the Guinness Book of Records as the brewer of Samichlaus, the strongest beer in the world (ABV 14 percent). In density, it is slightly inferior to its German rival, EKU 28. It would appear very difficult to brew a stronger beer, because the yeast which transforms sugars into alcohol (by fermentation) is in turn destroyed by the alcohol it produces. Only by carefully selecting strains of yeast which resist this death-by-alcohol, and by adopting a long conditioning process, have Hürlimann managed to produce so potent a beer.

First produced in 1979, Samichlaus is brewed each year on the feast of Saint Nicholas (6 December), from whom it derives its name, and is kept twelve months to the day before going on sale. There are two versions (both of equal potency), the lighter-coloured one being reserved for export. Drinking Samichlaus is an amazing experience: for a beer of such strength it is a great deal less sweet and heavy than one might expect, in some ways reminiscent of a brandy. It is in any case powerful in its effect and needs to be drunk slowly. It goes particularly well with the dried meat they produce in Graubünden canton.

flavour and not too sweet. Most of these beers are also available in draught form, which is becoming increasingly popular in Switzerland.

The merger of five breweries in the 1970s to form the Sibra-Holding group led to the creation of a single range of beers bearing the Cardinal label. The Cardinal brewery, founded in 1788 in Fribourg, is one of the oldest in the country, but only took on its modern-day structure in 1877, when it was acquired by the watchmaker Paul-Alcide Blancpain. Its present name dates from 1890, when it brewed a special beer to mark the accession of the bishop of Fribourg to the dignity of cardinal.

Its range includes a lager and a special beer (both available in brown and blond versions), a stronger brew called Rheingold (ABV 6.3 percent), and Moussy, an alcohol-free product. Cardinal also produces one of Switzerland's rare top-fermentation beers, Anker, a dark-amber coloured brew with a full, aromatic flavour (ABV 5.8 percent).

The other Swiss breweries produce beers in much the same mould, apart from Calanda (Chur) and Frauenfeld, which specialise in wheat-based brews. For the time being, beers of this type do not seem to have the same appeal as in Germany.

Basel has the distinction of housing one of the oldest micro-breweries in Europe, founded in 1974 by Hans Nidecker, who wanted to offer beers refused him by the brewers' cartel on the grounds that they were not produced in the canton. Nothing daunted, he decided to brew beer himself in his *Fischerstube* establishment. He now produces four beers: a fairly light blond; a brown with an alcohol content of 3.5 percent; a Weizenbier (ABV 4 percent); and Reverenz, a blond beer of similar strength. The food he serves – also cooked in beer – is worth making a special journey for.

AUSTRIA

Vienna, famous for waltzes and coffee with whipped cream, has also given its name to a style of beer. Light and refreshing, it had its time of glory in the last century, when it was imitated by brewers worldwide. Nowadays, if Michael Jackson is to be believed, it is no longer appreciated in Austria, and there is even some doubt as to whether this bottom-fermentation beer – rather sweet but less malty than its Bavarian counterpart – was in fact reddish amber in colour, or gold, as it still tended to be forty or so years ago.

It was first brewed in 1841 (just before the Czech Urquell pilsner) by Anton Dreher, one of the great names of European brewing in the last century, who ranks with the Bavarian Gabriel Sedlmayr or the Dane Jacob Christen Jacobsen. The new beer gave his brewery at Schwechat – founded in 1632 and bought by his family in 1796 – a new lease of life and led to the creation of subsidiaries in Bohemia, Hungary and Italy. The Dreher brewery at Trieste exists to this day.

Dreher's original brewery, near Vienna, is still in operation but, together with four other breweries, is now part of the country's main brewing group, Bräu AG, based in Linz. The Schwechat beers include various lagers – one bearing the name Hopfenperle but quite unrelated to the synonymous Swiss brand -and a premium beer known as Steffl. The group also produces Kaiser beers, the leading name on the national market and, at Salzburg, the highly-hopped Zipfer beers. Whereas Germany is known for bitter pilsners in the north and sweeter, more malty beers in Bavaria and the south, Austria specialises in fruity – even somewhat sugary – pilsners, which are nevertheless vigorous and full-bodied. This is especially true of Vienna. Typical examples are brewed by the Ottakringer brewery, the only independent company still operating in the Austrian capital. Founded in 1837 and owned by the Harmer family since 1938, Ottakringer has

made its Gold Fassl ('golden barrel') label the very epitome of an Austrian pilsner. It comes in standard (ABV 3.5 percent) and special (ABV 4.5 percent) versions, both superbly structured and beautifully finished. To celebrate its hundred and fiftieth anniversary, Ottakringer produced a fine old-style Viennese brew. Its other

products include a strong bock beer (ABV 5.8 percent) and a low-alcohol Helle (ABV 3.2 percent).

Steirerbrau, the other main Austrian group, came into being in 1977 with the fusion of several breweries: Reinighaus-Puntigam of Graz and Gösser of Loeben-Göss. The latter produces a rare phenomenon: Stiftsbräu, a syrupy brown beer which is nevertheless low in alcohol (ABV 3.6 percent).

In a country as mountainous as Austria, it is no surprise to find a white beer named Edelweiss: it is brewed by the Kaltenhausen brewery of Salzburg (a member of the Bräu AG group). Following the trend in neighbouring Bavaria, the taste for Weizenbier is also on the increase.

Another speciality of Salzburg is Columbus, a beer brewed by the Stigl brewery to celebrate two events which occurred in 1492: the discovery of America, and the foundation of the brewery itself! At Vorchdorf, not far from Salzburg, is the small Eggenberg brewery, which dates from the 17th century. It produces a number of much sought-after specialities, some of which are exported: Urbock 23, a hoppy and flavoursome blond with an alcohol content of 9.9 percent; Birell, a well-prepared alcohol-free beer; and, more recently, MacQueen's Nessie, a beer brewed from peat-smoked malt (ABV 7.5 percent). Nessie is an amazing, full-bodied tawny beer, rounded and well-balanced. Since being included in Heineken's World Beers range, it has made a name for itself on the international circuit. Austria also boasts an abbey which produces its own beers: the Premonstratensian monastery of Stägl in Upper Austria. Founded in 1580, it is famous for its March beer, one of several in its range.

FRANCE

In a country so committed to the production and enjoyment of wine, beer counts as something of a poor relation, underrated and often regarded as no more than a utilitarian thirst-quencher. Only the traditional beer-drinking regions (Alsace, Lorraine, the Vosges, Flanders, Artois) – which in any case belong more to the north of Europe than to the south – have maintained their brewing culture and practices. It was not always so: at one time breweries flourished all over the land from which sprang the Gauls and their *cervoise*. There were still more than three thousand of them at the turn of the century, and farm-breweries operated in the regions of Nice, Limoges, Toulouse and Brittany, as well as in the north of the country.

Industrialisation has led to most of them being swallowed up, overwhelmed by the superior productivity and commercial dynamism of the big firms operating in the eastern part of the country. Nowadays, less then thirty brewers are left: on the one hand, a few enormous industrial enterprises (the Heineken and two Kronenbourg plants at Schiltigheim in Alsace, Mons-en-Baroeul in the North, and Champigneulles); on the other, a number of medium and small-scale independents. Even so, all these brewers have something out of the ordinary in store for the questing beer drinker.

Recent years have seen a revival of interest among the French, whether in regional or foreign specialities, seasonal beers, or the products of micro-breweries.

Above: March beers have been reintroduced with great success by the Brasseurs de France, an organisation supported by all the main brewers.
Left: café waiters, an international symbol of beer in France, competing in their annual race through the streets of Paris.

ALSACE-LORRAINE

The east of France's cultural affinity with the German-speaking world, particularly evident in Alsace, goes a long way to explain why beer has always been held in honour in those parts, without for all that usurping the place of wine. Monks established breweries there at an early stage, and France's first lay brewer is recorded as having set up shop close to the cathedral in Strasbourg.

The reputation of Alsatian beers spread to Paris – and thence to the rest of France – in the wake of the industrial revolution,

The Kronenbourg brewery, which moved its premises to the Strasbourg suburb of Cronenbourg in

and the brewers of the region were quick to take advantage of the railways as a means of conveying their products to the capital. The disastrous war of 1870 and the occupation that followed, though it destroyed a number of local enterprises,

also led to exiles from the East setting up 'Alsatian' breweries in Paris. These popularised their refreshing and flavoursome bottom-fermentation beers, excellent when drunk with sauerkraut and pork-meat products. The two World Wars merely hastened moves towards concentration: the brewers of Eastern France, with their expertise and tradition, were best placed to take advantage of the inevitable disorganisation that follows such conflicts.

What is now the Alsatian style dates from the development of the bottom-fermentation process. The beer is only moderately hopped, and its alcohol content not normally in excess of 5 percent ABV. Kronenbourg products are undoubtedly the most widespread.

The history of the Kronenbourg brewery is typical of Alsace. It all began in 1664, when Jérôme Hatt brewed his first batch of beer in premises on the Place du Corbeau in Strasbourg. Before setting up his brewing enterprise, Hatt had obtained a diploma in cooperage and brewing, as was required at the time. In 1850 the firm's headquarters moved to a suburb of Strasbourg known as Cronenbourg, and the brewery experienced steady growth, its Tigre Bock being a great success. There was nothing to distinguish it from other breweries in the region until the post-war period, when another Jérôme Hatt first had the bright idea of packaging his beers

in 25-centilitre bottles. This innovation, combined with aggressive advertising, enabled him to win markets from his main rivals. The Hatt brewery, now renamed Kronenbourg (with a 'K'), was also quick to exploit the possibilities of supermarket sales, pioneering the concept of the throw-away bottle.

In 1970 the Kronenbourg breweries (a second giant plant had been built at Obernai) joined Antoine Riboud's BSN group, top dog of the agri-foodstuffs industry. They soon became France's market leader, accounting for almost a quarter of all sales with their two main beers: Kronenbourg and 1664.

The latter is a so-called 'special' beer, of a kind produced by all the main French brewers, stronger and more golden in colour than their standard product. It was first brewed in the 1960s to meet the requirements of café owners, who, seeing their prices controlled by the government, wanted another blond draught beer not subject to this restrictive regime. For the last couple of years, 1664 has been available in a brown version, also obtainable on draught.

The BSN group also controls the

Kanterbräu brewery with its two sites at Champigneulles in Lorraine and Rennes in Brittany. End result of a spate of take-overs that have characterised the brewing industry in Lorraine and other parts of France, Kanterbräu now produces a *bière de luxe* in its own name, a 'special' beer known as Gold, and a number of regional brews. It also deserves credit for having

launched France's first alcohol-free beer, Tourtel (which comes in blond, amber and brown versions). The name honours two illustrious French brewers of the last century, the brothers Prosper and Jules Tourtel, who at the time ran the biggest brewery in Lorraine, at Tantonville.

THE BREWING TOWN OF 'SCHILLICK'

There may be very few breweries left in France, but the small town of Schiltigheim (Schillick in the Alsatian dialect), near Strasbourg, is home to no less than four of them: Heineken (formerly the brasserie de l'Espérance), Fischer, Adelshoffen and Schutzenberger. Together, they provide employment for almost 2,000 people. The area meets the brewers' need for deep cellars safe from the floods that regularly wreak havoc in Strasbourg. Every summer, the town hosts a major beer festival, and its most prestigious restaurant, *l'Ange*, run by Ernest Wieser, is a mecca for those who enjoy foods cooked in beer.

In 1972, in an audacious move, the Dutch group Heineken took control of a cluster of Alsatian breweries, whose products included the old and highly-regarded Mutzig and Ancre labels. Advertising itself as the world's best-known brewer, the group, renamed 'Heineken breweries' in January 1993, has been through a process of massive reorganisation, involving the staged closure of a number of plants. The group now operates only three production facilities: at Schiltigheim in Alsace, at Mons-en-Baroeul, and outside Marseille. Dominated by the famous green bottle, the range includes over twenty brands, many of them regional, though some are now being phased out as part of a rationalisation programme.

Ardent advocates of modern marketing techniques at a time when competition from abroad is on the increase, the two Alsatian colossi are naturally aware of the danger of having only a single beer in their range. They have therefore created highly efficient integrated distribution networks and formed special arrangements with foreign brewers: Guinness and Carlsberg in the case of Kronenbourg; the Belgian Grimbergen in

the case of Kanterbräu. Meanwhile, in the last three years Heineken has created a range of foreign specialities under the name 'Bières du monde' (Beers of the world), which includes the Czech Urquell pilsner, the Mexican Corona, the alcohol-free Buckler, and the other great Dutch beer, Amstel.

In the shadow of these giants (BSN and Heineken account for over 60 percent of total beer sales in France), several independent brewers have managed to hold on in Alsace. Taking advantage of the long-standing regional market for authentic Alsatian beers, they also need to diversify and introduce some original products if they are to thrive and prosper.

The Pêcheur group, for instance, heir to an important part of Alsace's brewing heritage with its Fischer and Adelshoffen brands, has been conducting a creativity campaign under the leadership of its chairman Michel Debus, one of the most engaging figures in French brewing. Giant-killer of German protectionism in the European courts, he is a great creator of new beers. Having launched beer concentrate and a cherry-flavoured product, his group then introduced '3615', an aphrodisiac beer sold via the Minitel information network and, in more serious vein, Adelscott, a tawny-coloured beer brewed with peat-smoked malt of the kind used in making Scotch whisky. His next project is a rum-flavoured beer, to be known as Kingston!

At Hochfelden, a village which traces its brewing history back to the year 1000, the Météor brewery, itself over three hundred years old, capitalises on its 'image as a village brewery' in the time-honoured Alsatian tradition. Managed since the early years of the century by the Haag family, it brews a *bière de luxe* under its own name and two specials, one blond

Michel Debus, motive force of the Pêcheur group.

REMEMBERING THE PAST

In Lorraine and the Vosges, there are three museums to record the region's prestigious, but sadly defunct, brewing history. The most interesting is housed in an old malting at Stenay, a small town north of the Meuse. Its curator, Philippe Voluer, is one of the foremost French specialists in the history of European brewing and a visit to his museum is a real education.

The brewery at Saint-Nicolas-de-Port, in the Meurthe-et-Moselle department, closed down in 1985, but work to convert part of it into a museum is now nearing completion. The building itself is a superb example of industrial architecture at the beginning of the century, and well worth visiting for its own sake.

The third museum is at Ville-sur-Illon, in the Vosges, housed in another former brewery, which ceased production in 1975. It also bears witness to the region's once-flourishing brewing industry.

of Alsace, the local brewery has belonged for some years to the German Karlsberg group, whose own headquarters are only a few miles away, in the Saarland. With the input from Karlsberg, the Saverne

A cafe at the beginning of the century, rebuilt at the Musée de Stenay.

the other brown, bearing the Ackerland label. But the firm has also shown a penchant for innovation, marketing such new products as a 5-litre mini-keg, which gives customers the option of draught beer in the home, or a denser, fuller-bodied beer known as Mortimer.

Schutzenberger, the doyenne of Strasbourg breweries, celebrated its two hundred and fiftieth anniversary in 1990. 'Brasserie Royale' in the 18th century, 'Grande Brasserie de la Patrie' at the time of the Revolution, until the end of the Second World War Schutzenberger was managed by one of France's great brewing dynasties. It was then acquired by Charles Walter and is now run by his daughter, Rina Muller-Walter, the only woman boss of a brewing enterprise in Europe. With an almost obsessive concern

for quality, this brewery is one of the few in Alsace that continues to brew beers of high quality other then the traditional pilsners. In addition to Jubilator, a bottom-fermentation 'special', the range includes the remarkable Patriator, a brown beer akin to a German Double Bock; Schutz 2000, an unfiltered, bottle-conditioned beer first brewed to mark the two thousandth anniversary of Strasbourg's founding; and, more recently, Cuivrée, a sumptuous copper-hued beer (ABV 8 percent) to celebrate the brewery's two hundred and fiftieth year. Alcohol-free, March and Christmas beer also feature on its list, and Schutzenberger has even taken part in a project to create the 'Boisson de l'extrême', an alcohol-free restorative for sportsmen and astronauts.

At Saverne, a small town in the northeast

brewery and its leading brand, Fritz Bräu, have come a long way in the last few years, to the point where it was judged necessary to set up an entirely new brewery: an event so rare in French brewing as to merit special emphasis.

On the other hand, the group has been forced to close down the only brewery that remained to contest the supremacy of Champigneulles in Lorraine: Amos, of Metz, could no longer meet the current operational regulations. Grouped in their own association, the Alsace brewers are keen participants in Eurobière, the two-yearly beer exhibition held in Strasbourg.

MORTIMER, A STRONG BEER FROM THE MÉTÉOR STABLE

First unveiled at the 1993 Eurobière exhibition, the Alsatian brewery Météor's pure-malt Mortimer signals a deliberate break with tradition. With an alcohol content of 8 percent, this amber-coloured bottom-fermentation beer has a moderately hoppy flavour and plenty of fruit in the nose. Though its strength is not immediately apparent, this is a beer to sip slowly, rather like a liqueur. The impression is reinforced by clever packaging: the beer comes in a colourless, whisky-type bottle with a screw top, complete with an original drinking glass worthy of the finest pure malts. Mortimer is also available on draught.

CHRISTMAS AND MARCH BEERS

In recent years, the French have been rediscovering seasonal beers, and the brewers' experiments in this field have met with general success. Beers of this kind hark back to the days when brewing was more intimately linked with the cycle of the seasons, and the weather, on which depended the quality of the cereals and the success of the fermentation process.

Christmas beers (bières de Noël) have a longer history, and in the north of France the tradition has never really been broken. Brewed with the first fruits of the barley harvest (in September), the first

The brewing of March beers is a time-honoured tradition, as this diploma awarded to the Schutzenberger brewery in 1937 attests.

'good beer' was available for the end-of-year festivities, hence its name. As time went by, brewers would use the early barley to make a beer stronger than their run-of-the-mill pilsners, whilst offering it for sale at the normal price. This was the 'brewer's gift', made available to regular customers throughout the year.

Nowadays, Christmas beers are meeting with growing success, and all the northern French brewers, as well as a number from Alsace, have one on their list from the end of November. Heineken breweries are trying to establish the custom in Parisian cafés with their Sylver Christmas brew. These dense, amber-coloured beers go down a treat as a postscript to the evening meal.

More recently, French brewers generally have gone in for March beers, once the initial experiment pioneered by the Kanterbräu brewery had proved to be profitable. In the days of top fermentation, a March beer was brewed at the end of the year using the best barleys from the September harvest, which had by then undergone the complete malting cycle. After two full months maturing in cool conditions, the resulting beer, ready for the first warm days of spring, was reckoned to be the best of the whole year. Nowadays, industrial progress has

eliminated all these natural constraints but, by reviving this tradition, the Brewers' Association (Brasseurs de France) has found a way of imparting to consumers and the media a little of the brewing culture so sorely lacking at the present time.' As in the case of Beaujolais nouveau, the arrival of March beer is an event heralded by posters and advertising campaigns and stage-managed by enterprising café proprietors.

March beer is amber in colour but of only moderate alcohol content (ABV less than 5 percent). The essential thing is that it be fresh and clean on the palate. Working from a mutually-agreed standard, brewers are free to demonstrate their individual expertise and originality.

NORD – PAS-DE-CALAIS

In common with Alsace-Lorraine, the Nord and Pas-de-Calais are areas where beer still retains its supremacy, firmly anchored in the habits of everyday life. A number of brewers will still deliver their products direct to customers' homes, and beer continues to be the preferred drink in every café.

This is also the region with the highest concentration of breweries, ranging from small farm enterprises, which existed in their hundreds at the beginning of the century, to ultra-modern factories producing millions of hectolitres a year.

Flanders has a style of beer all its own: top-fermentation, dense, generally amber-coloured *bières de garde*, which the brewer leaves to mature for several months in his cellars before racking into bottles (usually 75-centilitre containers of the Champagne

type). Though akin to some of the Belgian abbey beers, this style is nevertheless quite specific, since Flanders *bières de garde* are sweeter and less malty in taste than those of other countries. These beers beg to be drunk in convivial surroundings, whether at home or in a café. They have staged a real comeback in the last twenty years, since the university students of Lille adopted Jenlain as their cult beer.

The brewers of the Nord area all offer a brown, fairly strong beer, which may be of top or bottom fermentation. As in Britain, brown beers were formerly drunk as a restorative by the workers of the industrial towns. Those brewed in this region, such as Pelforth brune or Porter

39, have a sweeter, less bitter flavour than their British counterparts.

The region's biggest brewery is located at Mons-en-Baroeul, near Lille. Owned by the Heineken group, it is the successor to a number of older firms that were forced to merge and produces some fine regional brands such as Pelforth (in blond and brown versions); Pélican (still sold in litre bottles with a spring stopper); Porter 39; and "33" Export. Recently modernised,

the Mons-en-Baroeul brewery has a bottling capacity almost without equal in France.

Another great brewery of the old school, the Motte-Cordonnier at Armentières, also near Lille, has one of the finest brewing halls in the region. Acquired by the Belgian Stella Artois group (now Interbrew), it is still producing bottom-fermentation regional beers, but not for long: it will soon be used only for conditioning the group's Belgian beers, brewed in its plants at Leuven and Jupille. The brewery houses a well-appointed little museum devoted to the topic of beer.

A third major group, the Brasserie de

Saint-Omer, is of more recent origin, combining the ancient Brasserie de la Semeuse and a smaller brewery at Boulogne. In addition to its common-or-garden pilsners, it offers some interesting specialities: Épi de Facon, one of the very few wheat beers produced in France; Réserve du brasseur, a flavoursome, amber *bière de garde* (ABV 7.5 percent); and Nordik, an exquisitely bitter blond, which has won a number of international awards.

At Roubaix, the Grande Brasserie moderne, a cooperative enterprise, is active in all sectors of the industry: a specialist in home delivery (70,000 customers served each week), it also brews to order for some of the big distributors and produces a brand of its own, Terken, available in both blond and

brown (or more exactly amber) versions. For almost twenty years, it has also been brewing Septante Cinq, a top-fermentation *bière de garde* (ABV 7.5 percent) quite typical of the genre.

Another worthy representative of the northern area's brewing heritage, the Jeanne d'Arc brewery at Ronchin depends heavily on a well-established network of customers, to whom it delivers beers for daily consumption. Its bottom-fermentation Orpal range can be safely classed among the general-distribution brands. This brewery also specialises in Christmas beers.

Finally, at Douai in Artois, the Enfants de Gayant brewery is named after the town's two 'Giants', huge effigies over three metres tall that are processed through the streets each year at carnival time. In addition to a range of classic lagers (Saaz and Goldenberg) for regional distribution, the firm, managed by Patrick d'Aubreby, one of the youngest brewers in France, has been a champion of innovation in the region. Its alcohol-free beer – Celta – was one of the first to go on sale in France (the manufacturing process was imported from Switzerland, where the Enfants de Gayant owns a brewery) and is one of the very few such beers available in draught

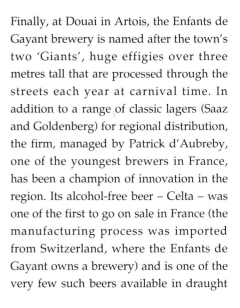

form. Its Bière du Démon is the strongest blond beer in the world (ABV 12 percent): a deceptive brew, its potency concealed under a velvety smoothness.

The Douai brewery's range also includes the attractive Bière du Désert (ABV 7 percent), sold in a whisky-type bottle. More recently, the brewery has signed an agreement to brew Saint Landelin, France's only true abbey beer, which was formerly produced by the monks of Crespin abbey. There are three versions of this top-fermentation brew: a blond (ABV 5.9 percent), an amber (ABV 6.8 percent) and a brown (ABV 6.2 percent) All three are distinguished by their subtle aroma and a well-rounded but delicate sweetness. Last but not least is the Douai brewery's Bière de Lutèce, a good example of a *bière de garde*.

In the Nord area, there are still a number of enthusiasts producing high-quality beers on a small scale. An outstanding example is the Duyck brewery, at Jenlain, not a stone's throw from the Belgian border, though 'small scale' is maybe no longer an appropriate term with production approaching 100,000 hectolitres. It is nevertheless still a true farm-brewery, set in the countryside, whose success has come from the rehabilitation of a top-fermentation *bière de garde*, known simply as Jenlain. It was the first beer to be packaged in champagne-type bottles, back in the 1950s. Nowadays, its reputation is such that it is even exported to Britain and the United States. Dark amber in colour, Jenlain is distinguished by a thick, creamy head and plenty of body. The same

Raymond Duyck, who by his promotion of Jenlain has opened up new markets to the bières de garde *of Northern France*

brewery's March beer – Bière du Printemps – is a golden brew with a taste that lingers agreeably on the palate.

In the heart of the old mining country, the more recently established Castelain brewery has applied modern technology (bottling in sterile conditions to avoid the need for pasteurisation) to top-fermentation beers. These include the fruity-flavoured Ch'ti, which comes in blond, amber and brown versions; Jade, brewed from guaranteed 'biological' barley malts, a fine, clean-tasting beer; and Réserve des Coulonneux, which is unfiltered and has a subtle aroma of yeast. At Saint-Sylvestre-Cappel, in the heart of French Flanders, Monsieur Ricour brews a magnificently complex *bière de garde* known as '3 Monts', and a great March beer. In the Valenciennes region, at Hordain, is another farm-brewery, where, come hell or high water, Alain Dhaussy maintains an ancient tradition with such *bières de garde* as Choulette, an amber, bottle-conditioned beer; Bière des Sans-Culottes, a golden blond which undergoes a secondary fermentation in the bottle; and, more recently, Abbaye de Vaucelles, a beer with astonishing honey overtones, no doubt similar to the 'prima melior' that the abbots of the Middle Ages had

brewed for their own consumption. On no account should this range of beers be missed.

Lastly, at Annoeullin, the 'La Maille' brewery offers a Pastor Ale, in imitation of products from across the Channel, and an exceptional beer known as Angélus,

Alain Dhaussy, master brewer of Hordain.

brewed from malted barley, wheat and rye. It has a superb complex flavour and lingering finish, combined with a remarkable freshness.

We could also mention Saint Léonard, Rince-Cochon and Colvert in trying to convey the richness and variety of the beers produced in Flanders and Artois. Their only drawback is that they continue to be little known and are brewed in small volumes. French beer drinkers are all too inclined to go looking abroad for specialities which, admirable though they may be, should not blind them to the fact that their own country has treasures undreamed of.

The Amis de la Bière, an association active in the region, is concerned to make them better known. It has the support of the Ghilde des Eswards-Cervoisiers, one of the rare confraternities devoted to beer (those that exist for the enjoyment of wine are legion). As well as organising promotional activities, it has sought to reinstate some of the old terms associated with beer, such as 'esward', the Flanders word for an inspector charged with quality control, 'goudalier', meaning a distributor, and 'cambier', once used to describe a brewer.

To promote its gastronomic specialities, the Nord-Pas-de-Calais region also awards a distinctive label to traditional products: *bières de garde* naturally occupy a privileged place, along with fine cheeses, bread and pork meat delicacies. In the Nord area, beer is the *sine qua non* of every festival, in particular the biggest of them all, the Grande Braderie, held in Lille at the beginning of September – a kind of huge car boot sale without the cars. For a whole weekend, the town is closed to motor vehicles and anyone can set up a stall on the pavement to sell the unwanted contents of cupboards and

attics. This event attracts between one and two million people, who also take the opportunity to enjoy the traditional dish of mussels and chips, washed down with plenty of beer, in particular Jenlain.

Beer also features prominently at carnival time. The Shrove Tuesday celebrations in

Dunkerque are a great occasion for people to dress up and let their hair down.

Big and small, the breweries of the Nord-Pas-de-Calais region are greatly in need of recognition from beer enthusiasts, for their circumstances are anything but easy: two were forced to close in 1992, and others have had to fight hard to resist

BEER-DRINKERS' CONFRATERNITIES

As well as the Amis de la Bière, France has a number of confraternities founded with the aim of championing beer: the Cervoisiers de France, based in Paris, which brings together a large number of café proprietors and brewery owners; the Chope d'or, a national organisation, founded to popularise beer-related gastronomy by organising dinners at which chefs serve special dishes cooked with beer; and the Houblon d'or, another body based in the Nord area.

economic pressures and the threat of take-over. Just as interest in beer is beginning to grow in France and in Europe generally, it would be a great shame if the Nord-Pas-de-Calais region were robbed of any part of its unique brewing heritage.

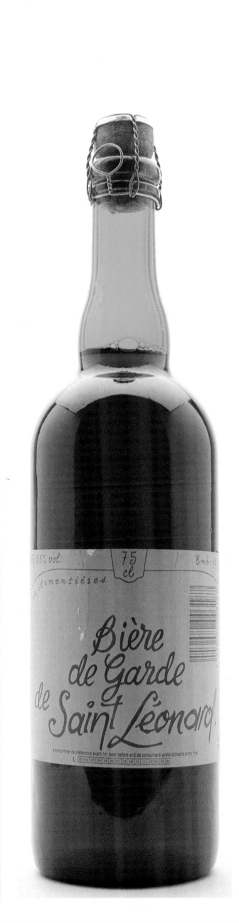

MICRO-BREWERIES

Britain, Germany and the United States have never really abandoned the practice of brewing beer for consumption on the premises, even though micro-breweries (or pub-breweries as they are often called) have staged a triumphant comeback in the last fifteen years.

In France, this is something quite novel, as the practice had long been defunct. The advantage of a micro-brewery is that it offers its customers a freshly-brewed product, unpasteurised and of a style quite different from the mass-produced beers on the market. The beer is brewed in full view of the public, which is also an effective educational exercise. With decor and menu suited to its beers, a micro-brewery can enjoy enviable success, provided that it is jealous of the quality and finish of the five or six products in its range.

After a somewhat shaky trial period in Paris, France's first real micro-brewery opened its doors in Lille five years ago under the name of *Les Brasseurs*. Its success was immediate, and led to the founding of a group inspired by the former owners of the Semeuse brewery. The aim was to implant similar businesses in other parts of France: Strasbourg, Mulhouse, Angers and Paris were the first links in the growing *Les Brasseurs* or *Taverne O'Neill* chain.

It is not essential to live in a traditional brewing area if you want to set up a micro-brewery. Indisputable proof of this is provided by Jean Michard's *Le Paris*, in Limoges. His full-bodied, rather sweet beers (including a Weisse in the authentic Munich style) have been a resounding success with the drinking public, and he sells three or four times the volume of beer dispensed in a year by the traditional cafés of the region. Built entirely of brick

and copper, the Limoges establishment is a delightful place for a drink and well worth a special visit.

The Spirit of Factory, a micro-brewery at Angers in the Loire valley, was designed and decorated in the American style on the advice of Peter Austin, who already has several dozen to his credit in different parts of the world.

German inspiration was behind the micro-brewery in Tours, which is combined with a restaurant and hotel. The

whole complex – complete with master brewer – was delivered, ready for operation, from across the Rhine.

Finally, Brittany boasts a micro-brewery of a slightly different kind, the *Brasserie des*

Micro-breweries have inspired a taste for beer in regions where it is not commonly drunk. Facing page: the Spirit of Factory, Angers; *this page:* le Paris, Limoges. *It is also possible to buy a complete kit for transforming one's bar into a micro-brewery (centre right).*

Deux-Rivières at Morlaix. Its beer, brand name Coreff, can be drunk at various venues in the region, which is not the usual practice with establishments of this kind.

Other projects are on the drawing board for different parts of France, as success obviously awaits these cafés with a difference. They pose no threat to their rivals. On the contrary, they are of benefit to the brewing industry in general, as they arouse a new interest in beer.

NORTHERN EUROPE

How does one explain the fact that, as far as beer is concerned, the countries of Northern Europe have experienced a worldwide expansion out of all proportion to their geographical size and political importance? Is it the memory of the Vikings of old, great drinkers and tireless rovers of the seas? Is it a logical consequence of the commercial acumen of the Dutch, among the first to open up new routes and establish trading posts? Or is it simply the limitations of their home markets that has led northern brewers to seek outlets abroad? Whatever the reasons, the Dutch Heineken and Danish Carlsberg groups are two of the biggest brewing concerns in the world, and have imposed their style of beer over vast areas. Of course, at home beer occupies a privileged place, and Danes and Dutchmen are near the top of the league table in terms of annual beer consumption. But their international expansion still remains something of an enigma, especially if we compare their success with the relative failure of the Germans, who have found many imitators for their styles of beer but have never really reaped the commercial rewards; or the British, who, despite the might of the Empire, have never gained general acceptance for their ales. Be that as it may, let us not forget that Northern Europe also has other beers to its credit besides Heineken and Carlsberg.

On a café terrace in Holland or among neighbours in a Danish garden: in Northern Europe, beer and conviviality go together.

THE NETHERLANDS

The Heineken saga is of relatively recent origin, though it is true that De Hooiberg ('the Hay Stack'), the original brewery acquired by Gerard Adriaan Heineken in 1864, dated from as far back as 1592. The young brewer's chief asset was his skill in ensuring the stability of his bottom-fermentation beer, which he named after himself. Right from the beginning, Heineken was keen to adopt new technology: in 1880, he commissioned one of the very first refrigeration systems, and he engaged a pupil of Louis Pasteur, the Frenchman Helion, to isolate a pure strain of yeast, which is still in use today. He was also one of the first brewers to venture into export markets, first shipping his products to France in 1880 and to the United States in 1933.

The characteristics of Heineken's pilsner beer are cleanness of taste, great stability and a certain blandness. This may well explain its international popularity, since it is agreeable to all and upsets no one. But it is certainly not the only pilsner beer of this type. Its success is due more to the financial and commercial genius of one man, Alfred Heineken, grandson of the founder. When he retired from the chair of the company in 1989, he left behind him a commercial empire built up over forty-seven years of tireless work.

Heineken found opportunities for expansion both at home (takeover of the rival Amstel brewery in 1968 and construction of Europe's biggest brewing plant at Zoeterwoude, with a production capacity of six million hectolitres per annum) and abroad. His first overseas brewery was set up in Burundi, in 1955, and that was only a beginning. Today, the group's beers are produced in fifty or so countries by over ninety breweries, some directly owned, others brewing under licence. The group is established worldwide: in Europe (where Heineken is the biggest brewer), it owns outright the Brasseries Heineken de France (which account for 25 percent of total French beer consumption) and has major holdings in

Spain, Italy, Britain, Greece and elsewhere; in Africa, it has a stake in thirty or so breweries; in Asia, it has interests in both China and Singapore. Even where Heineken does not actually own breweries, it remains a major exporter (to

at least one hundred and fifty countries), and its famous bottle with the green label undoubtedly ranks with Coca-Cola in international popularity.

This overseas expansion has transformed the little 'Hay Stack' into the world's second biggest brewing concern. Two years ago, Heineken drew ahead of the American Miller group, for many years second only to the colossus Anhauser Busch. Although its production volumes are double those of the Dutch group, it

must be said that almost all Busch's beer is brewed on American soil.

In the Netherlands themselves, Heineken produces close on seven million hectolitres a year, accounting for almost half of all sales. But its bottom-fermentation lager is not the group's only product: Heineken also comes in a brown version (known as 'Oud Bruin' in Flemish) and a Bok, a strong seasonal beer with an ABV rating of over 6 percent. For foreign markets, there is a brown Special

Alfred Heineken

HTB, THE HEINEKEN WATCHDOGS

Maintaining an identical style when your beer is produced in some eighty breweries around the world is no easy matter. But such is the task of the teams sent out by HTB (Heineken Technisch Beheer), a body of experts with few equals. As well as advising on the building and restoring of breweries in all parts of the world, and ensuring that the Heineken produced in the tropics is the same as that brewed in the Netherlands, HTB is also a major repository of documentation on beer and brewing. It helps all subsidiaries of the group to maintain the quality of their products, and intervenes whenever there is a technical problem. Safeguarding the environment (particularly the vexed question of getting rid of the waste water from the brewing process) is also part of its brief. Finally, HTB was instrumental in drawing up the blueprint for Buckler, the alcohol-free beer first marketed internationally by Heineken in the late 1980s.

Export brand. Amstel, too, is available in various guises: Light, Gold, Bock, Oud Bruin and 1870. Finally, the group continues to distribute brands it acquired in the past, such as Sleutel, Hooiberg and Van Hollenhoven (including a very interesting stout), whilst the De Ridder

brewery has maintained its autonomy. Though Heineken's original brewery in Amsterdam closed down in 1988, the group has replaced it with a micro-brewery.

This establishment is far from unique, with more and more being set up throughout the Netherlands. The most original, installed on the ground floor of a

windmill (where else?), where it produces top-fermentation beers in the abbey style, rejoices in the name of *'t Ij*.

Renowned for its bottle with the earthenware stopper, the independent Grolsch brewery derives its name from the ancient town of Grol (latterly Groenlo), near the German border, where it was founded in the 17th century by Peter Cuyper. One of the Netherlands' best pilsners, Grolsch is not pasteurised, not even for export purposes. The famous

bottle dates from 1898 and at one time there was talk of getting rid of it, as being more expensive than other forms of packaging. Nowadays, it is a magnificent selling point for the brewery, which fills more than 200 million of the bottles each year. Grolsch also has a second production facility, at Enschede.

The British Allied group owns two breweries in the Netherlands – Oranjeboom in Rotterdam and Drie Hoefijzers ('Three Horse Shoes') at Breda – producing several brands of lager. Oranjeboom sells well in export markets. Meanwhile, the Belgian Interbrew group has acquired the Dommels brewery, which produces a pale but strong pilsner

(ABV 6 percent) known as Dominator.

Holland also boasts the only Trappist brewery outside of Belgium: De Schaapskooi, at Tilburg in Brabant, founded in 1894. Following methods used by other Trappists – top fermentation, with yeast and sugar added during bottling to encourage a secondary action -the monks produce a range of three beers: a Double (ABV 6.5 percent), which, though dark, has a fine fresh aroma; a Triple (ABV 8 percent), more bitter and fruity; and a Quadruple (ABV 10 percent), a smooth, full-bodied beer, available only in the autumn after it has matured for a year. Served at between 12 and 16°C, these should be poured gently into the glass, so as to avoid mixing the sediment with the beer.

Established in 1870 at Schinen in Limburg province, the Alfa brewery still belongs to the heirs of its founder, Joseph Meens. It produces nothing but pure malt beers flavoured with whole hops. The brewery also has its own spring, 160 metres below the ground. As well as an excellent pilsner, Alfa brews a Dortmund-style lager with an alcohol content of 7 percent.

Limburg province and the town of Maastricht are home to a number of breweries, besides Alfa and De Ridder

(now a member of the Heineken group). Of these independents, Gulpener (in the little village of Gulpen) is one of the oldest, having been founded in 1825. It specialises in high-quality, unpasteurised lagers, the best known of which is X-perts. Gulpener also brews a Dortmund-type beer and, not long ago, revived a forgotten style – Mestreechs Aajt, or Old Maastricht – similar in some respects to the red (Rodenbach) beers of Belgium, which are matured for long periods in oaken casks. Low in alcohol and slightly

tart, this beer is an unrivalled thirst-quencher.

Not far from Maastricht, the firm of Brand takes pride in the fact that in 1971 it was granted the title of Royal Brewery by the queen of the Netherlands. It makes great play of this honour on its special, porcelain-type bottle. In addition to its rather bitter pilsners, the best known of which is Super Premium, Brand produces a wide range of beers, including German-style Bocks and a top-fermentation beer brewed only in the winter months.

Two small Dutch breweries have drawn inspiration from the Viennese style of beer, copper-coloured and full-bodied: De Kroon, of Brabant, brews Elegantier, while the Lindeboom brewery, in Limburg province, produces a beer known as Gouverneur. They also produce the more conventional pilsners.

DENMARK

During a dig in Denmark's Jutland peninsula, archaeologists discovered the tomb of a girl; beside her was a birch-bark bucket that had been used to hold beer. Analysis showed that the beer had been brewed with wheat and bilberries and flavoured with myrtle and honey. The recipe has long been lost, but it bears witness to Denmark's ancestral love of beer. The royal court already possessed its own brewery as far back as 1400.

In this country of barely five million souls, beer is something of a national institution, the two most famous brands – Carlsberg and Tuborg, now joined in a single enterprise – having opened a window on the wider world. Apart from the fact that their products are an integral part of daily life, for over a century these breweries have played a vital role in the economic, scientific and cultural life of the country.

Like the Bavarian Gabriel Sedlmayr and the Austrian Anton Dreher, the name of Jacob Christen Jacobsen is indissolubly linked with the development of beer in the last century and the revolutionary changes it underwent in just a few decades.

The Jacobsen dynasty was founded in 1801, when Christen Jacobsen arrived in Copenhagen from his native province of Jutland. A down-to-earth brewery worker, he showed such a talent for saving that, ten years later, he was able to rent a brewery on his own account. He already had an obvious penchant for scientific research, and was the first brewer to use a thermometer to regulate brewing operations. Conscious of the deficiencies of his profession, he enrolled his son, born in 1811, at the recently-founded Danish Polytechnic School, whilst having him work alongside him in the family brewery.

Jacob Christen Jacobsen became a great traveller, a rare phenomenon in those days, one of his journeys taking him to Bavaria, where he found the Spaten brewery engaged in its first attempts to master the bottom-fermentation process.

Completely convinced, he returned to Denmark with the process – and the yeasts needed for brewing Munich beers. The year was 1846. His efforts having found favour with the Danes, he built a new brewery outside Copenhagen and named it after his son Carl, born in 1842, adding the Danish word for a hill, *berg*. The Carlsberg brewery brewed its first batch of beer on 10 November 1847.

As sales increased, J.C. Jacobsen was reluctant to let the grass grow under his

feet and continued his search for new methods. In 1875 he set up a scientific laboratory and engaged the services of top specialists. One was Johan Kjeldahl, a chemist, who perfected a method, still in use, for determining nitrogen. Another was Emil Hansen, who completed the work of Louis Pasteur by preparing the

first pure culture of brewers' yeast, using a technique since adopted by all the breweries in the world.

For many years there were two Carlsberg breweries in Copenhagen, as Jacobsen had a second plant – the New Carlsberg brewery – built for his son. Whereas the father remained faithful to bottom-

fermentation beers on the Bavarian and Czech models, his son persisted in trying to brew top-fermentation, British-style ales, though without great success. All that now remains of his legacy is a stout, known as Gammel Carlsberg Porter. The two breweries were reunited in 1906. Their statutes are quite unique, since they belong to a foundation set up during his lifetime by J.C. Jacobsen, and their profits have been used to build up an impressive scientific, cultural and artistic heritage (see following pages). In 1970, Carlsberg merged with its long-standing competitor, Tuborg, the group thus formed now accounting for 80 percent of the Danish market. Each company has nonetheless retained its autonomy in the sales field.

It is in foreign markets, however, that the group's expansion has been most dramatic, with overseas sales – to over one hundred and thirty countries – three times greater than domestic turnover. Carlsberg and Tuborg own a number of breweries in Europe and Asia, and their beers are also brewed under licence.

The famous green label and logo (unchanged since it was designed in 1904) adorns a perfectly balanced pilsner (ABV 4.7 percent), often referred to as a 'Hof' by the Danes, whose remarkable cleanness of taste has proved to be a great asset in penetrating foreign markets. But the Carlsberg range also includes a number of other beers: Elephant, a pale golden colour, but considerably stronger (ABV 7.7 percent); Special Brew, which is reserved for export (ABV 8.9 percent); Gamle Øl, a brown beer in the Munich tradition; Imperial Carlsberg porter, a stout which, unlike its British original, is brewed by the bottom-fermentation process; 47, a fairly strong amber-

coloured beer (ABV 7 percent), whose name recalls the year of Carlsberg's foundation; and a number of lighter products such as Let (ABV 2.8 percent).

Though now making common cause with Carlsberg, Tuborg – established in 1873 –

was independent for almost a century. It is unique in having been conceived as an export beer: the brewery was sited on the dockside by its founders, a banker and a merchant. Modelled on a Bavarian beer, but paler and lighter than its rival Carlsberg, Tuborg was first marketed in 1875, after several years of preparation and research in Germany by master brewer Hans Bekkevold. The name is derived from a great 17th-century castle which once belonged to the wealthy merchant Jonas Thue.

At any early stage, new taxes on beer forced Carlsberg and Tuborg, though rivals, to enter into agreement to share profits and losses on an equal basis and pay over part of the profits to a charitable foundation. It would appear that this body has never lacked money ….

Tuborg's basic pilsner is commonly known as 'Green Tuborg'. The bottle is the subject of a giant monument dating from the last century, 26 metres high, which would hold the contents of over 1.5 million normal bottles. Other beers in the Tuborg range include Gold Label, a slightly stronger product (ABV 5.7 percent), which is widely exported; Classic, a darker, stronger beer first brewed in 1993 to mark the company's one hundred and twentieth anniversary; Julebryg, a Christmas beer, affectionately dubbed 'Snow beer' by the Danes, which is brought out in November; and Argansøl, a 'New Year's beer', which

differs slightly each year (the 1993 brew had an ABV rating of 9.3 percent). The label is always an original work by a well-known Danish artist. Further beers in the range are Red Tuborg (ABV 4.2 percent), a brown of Bavarian type; a blond with an alcohol content of under 3 percent; and a potent Easter beer (ABV 7.8 percent), a seasonal style much appreciated by the Danes. Since 1891, Tuborg has enjoyed the status of Royal Brewery, and one of its brands, Kongens Bryg, is a reference to this privilege. Tuborg is also known for a poster, *The Thirsty Man*, designed by the painter Henningsen, which in 1900 won second prize in a competition organised by the brewery. The picture became very popular, perfectly suggesting the pleasure of drinking a cool beer on a hot summer's day. It still features on the label of some half-litre bottles of the standard Tuborg pilsner.

In all, the Carlsberg-Tuborg group has at least twenty brands on the Danish market and for export, some of which are now brewed in its ultra-modern plant at Fredericia.

The 'New Year's beer' is brewed by Wiibroe, a subsidiary of the Carlsberg group since 1972. Founded in 1840 at

MAKING THE MOST OF THE BOTTLE

Although Danish pilsners are occasionally dispensed in draught form, the Danes are very attached to the traditional container, consuming an average of 380 bottles per head each year. In Denmark, drinking a toast consists in tapping your bottle against that of another drinker. Highly sensitive to environmental issues, the breweries do not produce non-returnable bottles. Some 99 percent of bottles are in fact returned, and it is rare to see a bottle left lying around; it is reckoned that each bottle is re-used at least thirty times. On the neck of its standard green bottle, Tuborg features 'Tuborgrammes': shorts texts of less than twenty words on newsworthy subjects, which, they say, are more assiduously read than newspaper headlines.

Elsinor – a town famous for its castle of Kronborg, the setting for Shakespeare's *Hamlet* – the brewery immediately specialised in lager-type beers. Cool cellars were required, and the founder, Carl Wiibroe, set up in the basement of the keep. For lack of space, his successors later moved to new premises, but for many years the brewery continued to offer a Hamlet beer, now alas defunct. Nowadays, Wiibroe brews a stout (ABV 6.5 percent), which is drunk in a cocktail with champagne (Black Velvet) or with lemon soda (Sea Foam); a lightweight pilsner (ABV 3.6 percent); and undoubtedly the weakest alcohol-free beer in the world: its alcohol content is a mere 0.05 percent. Brewed in the same way as a conventional lager, the alcohol is removed by a process specific to the brewery.

Another subsidiary of the Carlsberg group, Neptun, produces a unique, green-coloured beer, marketed each year at

Whitsuntide. Fairly strong, it is exported in some quantity to Japan and the United States. It is not the only *pinsebryg*, or Whitsun beer, but none of the others is green. With special beers for Christmas, the New Year, Easter and Whitsun, the Danes are decidedly well equipped for celebrating the major festivals.

Although pilsner beers are by far and away the predominant style in Denmark, there are still some top-fermentation brews, mainly of low alcohol content. One type is known as a 'white' beer, though it is in fact rather dark (Tuborg's Kongens Bryg – ABV 1.7 percent – is a good example), while the other is decidedly

pale in colour. Local in distribution and brewed mainly for festivals, they are classed as table beers and consequently are not heavily taxed.

Ceres and its subsidiary Thor form Denmark's second biggest brewing group, though even here Carlsberg has a finger in the pie. The group produces a

wide range of rather malty, typically Danish pilsners, but also a dark-coloured lager and a stout. Formerly, Ceres produced a rosé-tinted beer, but the colouring agent was banned when Denmark joined the European Community. A well-hopped brew, it still exists under the name of Red Eric – the Viking who discovered Greenland – but has become a more conventional blond.

The completely independent Faxe brewery, located to the south of Copenhagen, has been run as a family business since 1901. It has the advantage of its own, manganese-free water supply and has built its reputation on a medium-strength premium lager. This beer is filtered rather than pasteurised, which ensures greater freshness. Thirty percent of Faxe's production is now exported, mainly within Europe, in cans bearing the Great Dane label.

Another independent is the Albani brewery, established in 1859 on the island of Odense. It is noted for its stout and pilsners, and also brews a very strong pale lager called Giraf (ABV 6.9 percent), a slightly ironical reply to Carlsberg's famous Elephant, which is only a point or two stronger.

Of the smaller practitioners who make up the remainder of the Danish brewing industry, let us remember Hancok, which produces Old Gambrinus, one of the country's very few top-fermentation beers, akin to some Belgian specials in its density and coppery hue; and Maarebaek, whose Royal Viking, a strong, heady beer (ABV 9.2 percent), is exported to France for the enjoyment of the Artisans de la bière.

DENMARK'S CHARITABLE FOUNDATIONS

Jacob Christen Jacobsen and his son Carl, who set up the Carslberg foundations.

The Copenhagen Glyptotek (below) houses collections of both ancient and modern sculpture. Right: an Etruscan head; left: the Mother of Waters, *dating from 1920.*

Facing page: the famous Elephant Gateway to the Carlsberg brewery. Each is named after one of the founder's children.

The world-famous *Little Mermaid*, which since 1913 has sat watching the waters of Copenhagen harbour, was a gift from Carl Jacobsen, son of the brewing dynasty's founder. It symbolises the intimate relationship between beer and cultural life in Denmark, which takes the form of a complex system of charitable foundations almost unique in the brewing industry.

Willed by Jacob Christen Jacobsen during his lifetime, the foundations were to serve the interests of the business by encouraging scientific research in all possible fields. The Carlsberg Foundation, to which ownership of the business passed in 1888, on Jacob Christen's death, has three

and the protagonists of modern art. It also houses the Carlsberg Museum, which illustrates the history of the Jacobsen family. The first exhibit is the old wash copper in which Jacob Christen tried out the bottom-fermentation process on his return from Germany.

The Ny Carlsberg Foundation (whose offices are in the old Copenhagen town house where J.C. Jacobsen installed his first brewery) is active in all branches of the arts in Denmark. Its various forms of sponsorship are not limited to the fine arts and architecture, but extend to such fields as industrial design and public gardens. It regularly buys works from Danish artists to present to public or private institutions (schools, retirement homes, libraries, parks), and helps most of the country's museums to purchase works by world-famous artists. For instance, the Giacomettis, Henry Moores and Calders at the Louisiana Museum were acquired in this way.

The group's new breweries (at Fredericia in Jutland and Northampton in England) have won international prizes for the quality of their architecture, and the Ny Carlsberg Foundation has itself recently instituted an international prize, to be awarded on the advice of specialised magazines in this field.

In accordance with the terms of J.C. Jacobsen's will, the great man's house has become an honorary residence for 'any man or woman who has been of service to Danish science, literature or art', on the recommendation of the Danish Royal Academy of Sciences. The tenants to date have included the philosopher Harald Høffding, the physicist and Nobel Prize winner Niels Bohr, the archaeologist Johannes Brøndsted and the astronomer Bengt Strømgren.

Tuborg also supports a charitable foundation, set up in 1931, which has sponsored polar explorer Knud Rasmussen and physicist Niels Bohr, and has paid for the restoration of Viking drakkars found in Roskilde fjord.

stated objectives: to develop the Carlsberg Laboratory, established in 1875 and enlarged many times over the years; to subsidise Danish research in the fields of natural science, mathematics, philosophy (J.C. Jacobsen and his son Carl both held doctorates in this subject), human and social sciences by providing scholarships, paying the salaries of researchers, helping to equip laboratories, publishing scientific works, awarding prizes and financing archaeological exploration (for instance, the digs on the site of the Mausoleum of Halicarnassus); and, thirdly, to support the museum in the royal castle of Frederiksborg, which was restored by the highly patriotic J.C. Jacobsen and has

become the great repository of Danish natural history. Though mainly scientific in outlook, Jacob Christen also showed an interest in architecture: the 56-metre chimney of the Carlsberg brewery is in the form of a lotus flower, and around its base are replicas of the gargoyles gracing the cathedral of Notre-Dame in Paris.

More artistically inclined than his father, Carl Jacobsen, with his wife Ottilia, set up a second foundation, the Ny Carlsberg, or New Carlsberg, to sponsor the arts. Its greatest achievement is Copenhagen's Glyptotek, formed originally from Carl Jacobsen's personal collections of paintings and sculpture, ranging from the ancient Etruscans to the Impressionists

SCANDINAVIA

It takes some courage and determination to be a brewer in the Scandinavian countries, as politicians and church leaders regularly point to beer as the cause of alcoholism and all the country's moral ills. The production and sale of beer is strictly controlled and restricted by swingeing taxes and more or less open prohibitions on certain types of beer. This is true in Norway, Sweden, Finland and, not least, Iceland, where until recently it was forbidden to brew any beer with an alcohol content of over 2.25 percent or import any foreign beers exceeding this figure.

It must be the memory of the ancient Vikings, whose image as great beer drinkers is associated with tales of brigandage and Gargantuan feasts, that provokes the latent puritanism of the northern peoples and leads to such severe restrictions on alcohol – with beer the first victim.

Beers are classified into a number of categories according to their alcohol content, with a very high level of tax on so-called strong beers (this category begins at 3 percent and may not exceed 4.5 percent!). The sale of these beers, together with wines and spirits, is generally limited to state-monopoly shops and to restaurants, where the prices bear no relation to manufacturing costs.

Despite these measures, which amount to prohibition in another guise, there has been a modest increase in beer consumption in recent years and a growing interest in more original beers, whether produced in Scandinavia or imported from abroad.

In Sweden, it was as recently as 1955 that the sale of class III 'strong' beers (i.e. between 3 and 4.5 percent ABV) was limited to state shops. This proved to be the *coup de grace* for most of the hundred and twenty breweries existing at the time. The remaining brewers then switched their efforts to beers of 'medium' strength (*Mellanøl*), with an ABV rating of around 3.6 percent. Their success enraged the anti-alcohol lobby which, interpreting it as a threat to young people, managed to have this category suppressed by Parliament in 1977. The beer now sold over the counter at normal prices may not exceed 3.6 percent ABV, which does not leave the brewers much room for originality or inventiveness.

Of course, the breweries are still allowed to produce stronger beers, but these must be sold at high prices and only through the state network of outlets (*Systembolaget*), whose opening hours are most inconvenient. Alternatively, they may be exported. All these restrictions have tended to concentrate the brewing industry in a few hands, with three groups accounting for 90 percent of total turnover within Sweden. The remaining

10 percent consists of imported beers and the products of a few smaller breweries. Each of the major groups has also had to diversify into soft drinks and mineral waters in order to maintain its sales volumes.

Pripps, Sweden's biggest brewing concern, derives its name from Joan Albrecht Pripp, who acquired an old Göteborg brewery in 1828. He and his son Carl expanded the business, which eventually merged with its local rival, Lyckholm. Meanwhile, in the capital, the twenty or so firms existing at the turn of the century had joined forces to form a single entity, the Stockholm Breweries. The inevitable eventually happened, and in 1964 the two groups became one. The new conglomerate kept the name of Pripps in its title, finally becoming Pripps Breweries in 1972. This was all done at the behest of the Swedish state, which is still a

shareholder in the agri-foodstuffs company Procordia, joint owners – with Volvo – of Pripps Breweries.

Pripps Blå continues to be the group's most popular brand, accounting for 25 percent of the Swedish market. It is a classic lager, of only moderate strength to comply with the rigours of the Swedish classification, which consists of three categories defined by law. This brand is produced in a wide variety of forms, such as Pripps Fat (a diet beer), a Pils, a Special Lager (sold mainly on draught), and a dryer, more bitter Special Brew, recently introduced in a new-style bottle for the benefit of the catering trade. The group also produces Julöl, a brown, fairly strong Christmas beer.

Three Towns (a reference to Sweden's three principal cities of Stockholm, Göteborg and Malmö) was for many years a popular beer but, after falling victim to the move to suppress the medium-strength category, is now produced mainly for export. There is also a beer known as Three Hearts, again an export product, brewed by a small firm near Göteborg: the similarity in name, if not in taste, is striking.

Although Pripps concentrates mainly on its leading brand, it does have other strings to its bow. The most original is its Carnegie Porter, also Sweden's oldest

label. It dates back to 1836, when a young brewer of Scots origin, David Carnegie, settled in Göteborg and began producing beers in the Scottish style. A gold medal winner at Burton upon Trent in 1992 (a rare accolade for a foreign stout from the British judges), Carnegie Porter comes in two versions, both produced by the top-fermentation process: the more common is of medium strength (2.8 percent ABV); the second, slightly stronger, has been produced annually since 1985 and is kept for eighteen months before being released onto the market. The brand's reputation has encouraged Pripps to use the name to sell a low-alcohol lager.

Grängesberg, an old independent brewery, survived the suppression of the 'medium-strength' category by joining forces with two other firms and reviving the old family name of Spendrup. Since reorganisation, it has concentrated on two pure malt beers: Premium, a well-hopped product which exists in standard and strong versions; and the even more hoppy Old Gold (classed as a strong beer).

Falken Breweries, a subsidiary of the agri-foodstuffs group Unilever, features a falcon as its trade mark. Set up in 1896, the firm founded its reputation on a spring of pure water located at Falkenberg, where the brewery stands to this day. Its leading brand, Falcon Export,

is a moderately bitter lager of conventional type, but the group also produces a wide range of other beers: Falcon Bayerskt, a full-bodied, amber-coloured beer, brewed with dark malts, which comes in standard and strong versions; Falkenberger, a lighter, rather malty beer in the German Dortmund style; Gammelbrygd, a vintage product packaged in an opaque bottle and sold with its own opener, which is akin to a porter and, though not over-strong, has the aroma of an old port wine; Julöl, a slightly sugary brown Christmas beer; Kaltenberg, a pale, Bavarian-style lager, of which there is also a dark version known as König Ludwig. This beer is also available on draught, as are Falcon Export and Bayerskt.

The group also controls the Till brewery, once famous for mead and a beer flavoured with juniper berries. Nowadays, it produces a range of fairly conventional lagers.

As well as classifying its beers into four categories, a decade or so ago Norway began imposing even higher taxes on beer than on wines and spirits. This tended to discourage consumption of beers stronger than 4.5 percent ABV, reinforcing the predominance of the pilsner type. It is also possible to find seasonal beers (particularly for Christmas and summer drinking) and derivatives of the Bavarian and Dortmund styles.

Norway's biggest brewing concern is the Noral group, whose Ringnes and Frydenlund breweries in Oslo produce some well-hopped beers.

The country's oldest brewery is in the nearby town of Drammen. The firm of Aass (pronounced 'os'!) dates back to 1834 and has been owned by the same family for over a century. Its fame is due to a Bock beer, which won a medal in Paris in 1900, though the range also includes ten or so other products, some packaged in magnificent bottles for export.

Each of the chief Norwegian towns still has its own brewery: Hansa in Bergen, Tou in Stavanger, Mack in Tromsø. The

latter is situated 300 kilometres inside the Arctic Circle, making it the most northerly brewery in the world. Its Arctic Beer exports well on account of its curiosity value.

In Finland, beer, having superseded grain-based spirits in popular favour in the 19th century, became the target of full-scale prohibition in the 1920s. As a result, its manufacture and distribution became

concentrated in the hands of the state. The monopoly was relaxed in 1969, but all brewers have to conclude an agreement with the state agency, which is alone entitled to distribute 'strong' beers of over 4 percent ABV. A tax of 40 percent is applied to these products, value-added tax adds a further 16 percent to the price. Despite these drawbacks, four groups, representing a dozen or so breweries, manage to thrive. Hartwall, Finland's biggest brewer, produces a relatively-strong, golden-coloured Lapland lager, known as Lapin Kulta (5.3 percent ABV), two other pilsners (Aura and Karjala) and a wheat-based beer derived from an Austrian model.

The range of the Pyynikki group (brand name Amiraali) includes beers from a brewery of Russian origin (Synebrichoff), as well as a British-style porter and an ale. Finland has maintained the tradition of home brewing: sahti is prepared using malted barley and rye, then flavoured with juniper berries.

CENTRAL EUROPE

The collapse of the region's communist regimes has made the beers of Eastern Europe more accessible to the intrepid enthusiast. Until quite recently, Urquell and Budweiser – the renowned Czech pilsners – were the only brands with any following in the West. Of the former Czechoslovakia's breweries, the lion's share are located in what is now the Czech Republic, though Slovakia also has some fine beers among its assets: Goldener Fasan, brewed in Hurbanovo; Tatran, from Poprad; or the strong Martinsky Porter (ABV in excess of 7 percent), which has a distinct taste of burnt malt.

Each historical region has its own brewing traditions. Bohemia, for instance, has a reputation for high-quality brown beers, with notable examples produced in Stankov, Krusovice and Chodova, while the town of Velké Popovice brews the very malty Kozel brand. The general deterioration of the economy has prevented these breweries from investing in modern technology and equipment, with the result that quality has suffered. They are now trying to make up the leeway with the assistance of their counterparts in the West, who are of course keen to get a foothold in such promising markets: beer is a popular drink with many of the peoples of Central and Eastern Europe.

Above: fermentation of Urquell Pilsen, the beer which gave its name to pilsners the world over.

Left: bar in a Czech working-class district. Here, beer is an essential feature of daily life.

THE CZECH REPUBLIC AND SLOVAKIA

The quality of the barleys grown in the plains of Moravia and the Elbe, the fine, spicy flavour of the hops cultivated around Zatec (Saaz in German) and Ustek – highly regarded on the world market – long ago established Bohemia as a centre of excellence in the world of brewing. Hops have been grown in this region for over a thousand years and the brewers of those far-off days were undoubtedly the first to use them as a flavouring for their

beers. Guilds of maltsters sprang up in Prague in the early 14th century and the brewers, too, as their numbers increased, formed themselves into powerful corporations.

A concern to improve quality is evident in the regulations promulgated towards the end of the Middle Ages, and one of the very first technical books on beer was published in 1585 by the Czech Tadeas Hajek. When technological innovation began to revolutionise all aspects of brewing in the 19th century, the maltster Frantisek Poupé was pre-eminent in organising his activities along scientific lines.

While the Jecmen brothers were laying the foundations of the Czech bottom-fermentation process, in 1830 professor Balling of Prague university set about studying enzymes, acquiring knowledge vital to our understanding of what goes on during fermentation; named after him, the Balling scale is used for measuring the density of worts.

Sharing the honours with Vienna and Munich, Bohemia was the first region to adopt the bottom-fermentation process. In 1842, the brewers of Plzen (Pilsen) – site of a brewery since the late 15th century – finally settled on a golden-coloured beer, well-hopped (400 g/hl) and with a generous head. Their Urquell Pilsen quickly became the international standard of reference, the ancestor of all pilsner beers.

The Plensky Prazoroj brewery still exists, one of the glories of the Czech Republic, and a valuable source of foreign exchange. Extremely low in mineral salts, the local water is very soft, which means that a large amount of hops can be added to the wort, imparting a good, hoppy flavour to the beer without excessive bitterness. Urquell is matured in open wooden vats at a constant temperature of around 0 °C. The carefully maintained storage vessels are housed in cellars cut from the living rock. The spicy aroma of this beer is quite remarkable, especially when served in draught form.

After the fall of the socialist regime, when

privatisation was the order of the day, foreign brewers (in particular Heineken and Grolsch) tried to gain control of the Pilsen brewery but, inspired by popular sentiment, town and government made valiant efforts to ensure that this national treasure remained in Czech hands.

Gambrinus, another Pilsen brewery, produces a beer which merits equal status with its more famous neighbour.

Another town renowned for its beers is Ceské Budejovice, formerly known as Budweis, which explains the name of its main product, Budweiser, brewed by the Budvar company. Budweiser is also the name of America's leading brand of beer, brewed for over a century by Anheuser-Busch, and a dispute rumbles on as to which of the two companies is really entitled to use the designation. Czech Budweiser is distinctly fruitier than its Pilsen rival.

Great drinkers (almost on a par with the Germans), the Czechs can enjoy some excellent, mostly blond, beers in nearly all their main towns, not least Prague: Staropramen's Smichov is a great classic, as are the beers of the Branik brewery. Prague must rank with Munich in the mind of the questing beer drinker. Its oldest tavern, *U Fleku*, dates from the 15th century, and beer is still brewed on the premises, notably an amber-coloured speciality.

Other interesting Czech products include the 'biological' beers of Karlovy Vary (formerly Karlsbad); the Brensky Drag ('dragon'), Jezek and Starobrno brands produced in Brno; and the beers brewed by the Radegast and Ostravar companies of Ostrava. Although none of these is exported at the present time, those privileged to have tasted them are unanimous in extolling their virtues and the subtle variations of hops and malt they exemplify.

Do not be put off by the apparently excessive strength of Czech beers as indicated on their labels: the Balling scale is still used for measuring the density of the wort, and 12/13 degrees Balling correspond to an ABV rating of around 5 percent.

HUNGARY

Hungary's former association with the Austrian empire was a key factor in the way the brewing industry developed there. The Austrian Anton Dreher, creator of the Viennese style in the last century, also founded one of Hungary's main

breweries, the Kobanya, which is still active today. The country's brewing industry is more concentrated than that of its neighbours, with just seven breweries controlling the market. Five of them in fact account for 90 percent of current production. The market has been growing since economic activity was deregulated, with annual consumption increasing from about 10 litres per head forty years ago to 95 litres at the present time. The brewers are now well placed to meet the demand, offering a fairly wide range of bottom-fermentation, pure malt beers.

A good example, from Budapest, is the Kobanya brewery's Rocky Cellar, an oblique allusion to its founder, Anton Dreher, who for maturing his beers used the underground quarries from which rock had been extracted to build the town. Other brands from this brewery include Hungaria, Budapest, Kobanyai, and Bak, a dark-coloured Bock with an ABV rating of over 7 percent.

The Kanizsa brewery, located in the town of Nagy-kanizsa, where it has always been associated with a malting, celebrated its centenary in 1992. Brewing was interrupted for many years during and after the Second World War, and production did not begin again until 1957. In 1984 Kanizsa entered into a joint-venture agreement with the Holsten brewery of Hamburg, whose beers it also brews under licence. The partnership has resulted in considerable technical improvements. Best known for its Siraly brand, a blond lager featuring a seagull on the label, Kanizsa also produces a number of other beers, including the slightly stronger Korona and a brown known as Göcseji Barna. In 1991 total production was in excess of 1.2 million hectolitres.

Holsten is not the only western company to have taken an interest in the Hungarian market, far from it. In late 1991, the Belgian Interbrew group acquired a majority holding in Borsodi, the country's second biggest brewing concern, which sells over 3.2 million hectolitres a year of its Vilagos, Rakoczi and Barton brands. Borsodi's Premium is now being intensively promoted by the Belgian group through its beer cellar network.

The Dutch giant, Heineken, was almost bound to follow suit and has since gained control of the Komaromi brewery near Budapest, intending to brew its Amstel brand in situ. Hungary imposes fairly severe import quotas, so foreign brewers seeking to make an impact on the market are effectively obliged to buy up local breweries and brew and distribute their products on the spot. Finally, the Austrian Brau AG group has bagged a brace of Hungarian breweries: Martfu and Sopron.

The list of foreign take-overs is quite likely to grow, with many Western brewing concerns looking to Hungary as a promising new market.

RUSSIA

Kwasz, the traditional drink of the Russian peasant, was brewed on the farm from rye – sometimes mixed with wheat and barley – and sweetened to taste with fruits (particularly bilberries). It was low in alcohol and had little in the way of a head. Though various attempts were made to produce *kwasz* on an industrial scale, during the 19th century it gradually gave ground to barley-based beers, production of which was in any case more easily controlled by the authorities. The main breweries of Moscow, St. Petersburg, Kiev and Kharkov date from the last century, and in 1913 there were more than a thousand of them, producing 11 million hectolitres a year. The Revolution and the two World Wars concentrated production to some extent, though the prohibitive cost of transport has militated against excessive centralisation.

A great deal of beer is consumed, though there was a serious set-back in 1985, when new laws to combat alcoholism were introduced, and growth has been consistently hindered by a lack of new investment.

Traditionally, Russia produces two categories of bottom-fermentation beer: light blonds, such as the Leningrad, Moscow and Neva brands, to which rice flour is sometimes added; and browns, which have something in common with British porters and are very low in alcohol: typical is the malty Velours (ABV 3 percent). Some brands are exported, for instance Zhiguli (which also enjoys national coverage) or Riga, but most of the sixty or so national brands (not to mention the many purely local brews) have yet to be discovered.

The beers of other former Iron-curtain countries are widely known. Though drunk in some quantity, the beer produced in Romania and Bulgaria is not available abroad, and even at home production is limited by a lack of bottles and of (generally wooden) storage casks.

POLAND

Though beer has been popular since the Middle Ages, when it first established its place in local traditions and religious festivals, in the last century it lost ground to vodka, which eventually became the national drink. Poland's low per-capita consumption is, however, due mainly to the incapacity of local breweries to satisfy demand, as their facilities are often antiquated (some of the equipment still in use is said to be over a century old). Production is in the hands of 24

companies operating some 80 breweries, and since Poland opened its doors to investment from the West there have been some big changes. According to one Polish specialist, even a doubling of production would not be sufficient to satisfy demand but, to protect the home market, the government has imposed heavy customs duties on foreign beers. Moreover, beers of all classes are hard hit by the campaign against alcoholism, which makes them expensive for the average consumer.

The bulk of the beer brewed is of the pilsner type and of relatively low alcoholic strength, though the country also produces some Munich-style brown beers, and strong dark porters (ABV 7 percent and over) have been drunk on the shores of the Baltic for over a century. Small quantities of top-fermentation beer are also produced, by the Grodzisk Wiekopolski brewery, using an old recipe involving smoked, malted wheat.

Polish beer is rarely pasteurised and does not keep or travel well. For this reason, most beers are drunk within a radius of 30 km of their brewery of origin. Only the

Okocim brewery, located in the town of that name and more modern than its competitors, is able to produce an unpasteurised beer that will keep. The Okocim and Pozan breweries are in fact the biggest in the country. Privatisation is therefore seen by most breweries as their chief hope of obtaining much-needed

investment. The operation began two years ago and involved the country's main breweries: Okocim, Zywiec (whose pilsner is the beer most exported to the West, particularly to countries with strong Polish communities), and Kozalin. Interests in brewing have been acquired by the Poles themselves and by foreign

THE PBP (POLISH BEER-DRINKERS PARTY)

Poland's new-found political freedom has given rise to an organisation that must be unique: the Beer-drinkers Party. Initially intended as a joke, the strongly nationalist party now holds a number of seats in parliament and campaigns for the deregulation of the trade in beer and other products. Many of its members are ambitious to obtain licences to sell beer in bars and restaurants.

In its weekly newspaper, *Kurier Piwny*, the party has published a quality classification of Polish beers. The leading brands are listed as Magnat (Wroclaw), Kaper Krolewski (Gdansk), Zagloba (Okocim), Piast (Wroclaw), Kanclerz (Slupsk) and Glubczyce (from the town of that name).

companies. The Australian group Brewpole, for instance, gained control of the Gdansk (Danzig) and Elblag breweries, and the big Heineken, Interbrew and Carlsberg groups have been looking for partners with whom to set up joint ventures. By law, they can acquire only minority holdings. Other breweries are being privatised at Szczecin, Wroclaw, Poznan and Lublin. Despite its financial difficulties, Poland intends to retain title to its breweries wherever possible. According to the minister responsible for privatisation, 'the aim is not to produce DAB in Poland instead of Zywiec, but to create a situation in which Zywiec sells better than DAB'.

THE MEDITERRANEAN LANDS

In the warm Mediterranean sunshine, wine has always been the privileged drink of gods and men. In referring to beer, the Roman commentators were nonplussed: their use of the term 'barley wine' speaks volumes for the lowly place it held in their esteem.

By making wine, with bread, the great symbol of Christ's sacrifice, the Christian religion reinforced this tendency. It is true that monks have brewed beer since the Middle Ages, but it was for their everyday requirements and to meet the needs of common pilgrims; for high days and holidays, they brought out the wine. The Muslim religion, for its part, condemns the use of any form of alcohol, consigning beer and wine to hell without distinction.

Against such a background, it has been difficult for beer to win a place in the sun, especially as the Mediterranean heat makes brewing a complicated and chancy business. Not until the technological revolution of the last century did a brewing industry really become established, and then under the guiding hand of brewers from Germany, Austria and France.

Although, with very few exceptions, the Mediterranean countries are lacking in authentic traditions and original styles of beer, there has been a growth in demand in the last ten or twenty years. Could it be the influence of holiday-makers from the North, who invade the Mediterranean beaches and expect to find their favourite drink to hand? An interesting theory, but a more likely explanation is the internationalisation – or at least the Europeanisation – of the way people live. Except in Italy, the production and consumption of beer is on the increase, under the ever tighter control of multinational groups, which are bringing all their brewing and marketing expertise to bear.

Left: the much-frequented harbour of St Tropez, its row of café terraces fronting the Mediterranean.
Above: Barcelona's bodega Barrio Chino. Spanish cafés of this type serve both wine and beer.

SPAIN

The emperor Charles V, born in 16th-century Flanders, is the subject of several anecdotes relating to beer; anecdotes still recounted in Belgium. He was also king of Spain, which is why, during his reign, some of his German retainers set up the first breweries recorded in the Iberian peninsula. Vestiges of their influence remain: for instance, the Damm brewery still uses gothic characters on its labels and even calls its beers Voll-Damm. But it is equally possible that this is a marketing ploy to attract the German tourists who descend in hordes each year on the beaches of the Costa del Sol.

Damm, which owns breweries in Barcelona, Valencia, Murcia and Grenada, is actually the only Spanish brewer to have maintained its independence. On account of its Catalan credentials, Damm was chosen as the official beer for the 1992 Olympic Games, and because it was able to offer the athletes an alcohol-free beer, inappropriately known as Sin! The other breweries succumbed long ago to the European giants, who have gradually

tightened their grip on the industry.

It must be said that Spain presents an attractive proposition. Whereas in northern Europe there has been no significant increase in beer consumption for decades, the Spanish market has been in continual expansion for the last twenty years. Consumption per head currently stands at 72 litres, as compared with a figure of 40 or so for France. In fact, the total volume of beer produced in Spain now exceeds that of Belgium or Czechoslovakia.

The influence and thirst of foreign tourists are no longer sufficient explanation for the high consumption figures. Beer has become an essential element in the feverish night life of Madrid or Barcelona.

Hoegaarden, the white beer from Flanders, is currently all the rage: the emperor Charles V would have approved! All this has led to fierce competition. The various Spanish breweries are running more or less neck-and-neck, with changing trends and new alliances creating a very fluid situation. San Miguel, for many years the top brewing

concern, has recently been forced into second place by Aguila, but the recent takeover of Union Cervecera by Cruz del Campo – under the auspices of the British giant Guinness – could soon bring about another change in the order.

Located in Madrid, the El Aguila brewery is owned 100 percent by the Heineken group. It brews a number of lager-type beers in its own name, as well as the more German-sounding Adlerbrau. The Dutch group's special interest in its subsidiary is attested by the fact that, in 1988, El Aguila was chosen to run a trial of the new alcohol-free Buckler beer before it went on sale in the rest of Europe.

Mahou, another major brewer, is 33 percent owned by the French BSN group. BSN also has a stake in San Miguel, which has retained its links with the Filipino group of the same name. San Miguel puts the accent more on quality, brewing slightly stronger lagers. These include a pilsner with an alcohol content of 5.4 percent and Selecta, a smooth, special brew.

The Danes, too, have a finger in this pie: Carlsberg holds shares in Cruz del Campo, based in Seville, where a new brewery has recently come on stream. Although blond lagers account for most of the beer consumed in Spain, there are also some darker, stronger beers. Notable examples are Voll-Damm, already mentioned, and Ambar Export, from Saragossa.

PORTUGAL

Like Spain, Portugal has seen a rapid increase in beer drinking: over the last five years, per capita consumption has increased from 47 to just over 67 litres per annum. But here the similarities end. Breweries were founded in Portugal in the 19th century, but they have always operated in isolation: the volume of both imports and exports is very low, especially considering the growth in the market.

The brewing industry is now dominated by two rival groups. The bigger of the two, the Lisbon-based Central de Cervejas, is best known for its nationally-distributed Sagres brand, available in blond and brown versions. When Portugal was admitted to the European Community, the brewery had the bright idea of producing an export beer named Europa, the first to bear this name. Central de cervejas also brews small quantities of a top-fermentation beer, known as Bohemia.

Its eternal rival, Unicer (a shorted form of Uniao Cervejeira), is based in Oporto. When the economy was privatised in 1991, the formerly nationalised company entered into a joint venture with the Carlsberg group. It now operates three modern plants.

The island of Madeira has its own small brewery.

ITALY

Where beer is concerned, Italy is truly the 'sick man' of Southern Europe. Whereas the other countries in the region have increased their consumption, the annual par capita figure for Italy remains low: just 22.4 litres. Italy is in fact bottom of the European – and world – league table, strange in view of the country's relatively high standard of living. And in recent years the situation has been one of stagnation, even decline.

Of course, the peninsula is far better known for its wines, but beer is certainly no novelty. The great Austrian brewer Anton Dreher introduced his beers to the region over a century ago, and in Milan there is still a brewery bearing his name. Owned 100 percent by the Heineken group, it also controls the Sicilian Messina brewery, whose blond lager enjoys international distribution as one of Heineken's 'World Beers' range.

Like the Spaniards, the Italians have developed a taste for foreign beers, and Italy is therefore an interesting prospect for European brewing concerns. Those that have made major investments include the French Kronenbourg group, which has a minority holding in Peroni, the market leader. Peroni's best-known product is the classic Nastro Azzurro lager. The group also owns the Raffo trade mark.

Wuhrer, another Italian brewery with a German-sounding name, was set up in the last century by the Bavarian Heinrich von Wunster. For many years a family business, this brewery is now a subsidiary of the Belgian Interbrew group. Its leading brand is Classica von Wunster.

Founded in 1877, the Poretti company, which owns breweries in Varese and, South of Rome, at Ceccano, now belongs to Carlsberg. It markets a number of beers bearing the Splügen label: a relatively strong lager, a German-style Bock and, in more recent times, a coppery-red smoked beer reminiscent of those brewed in Northern Bavaria.

Since the 1940s, the Moretti label has featured a behatted man with a moustache about to drink from a brimming mug of fine, amber-coloured beer. Moretti, founded in Udine as far back as 1859, was also for many years a family business but is now a subsidiary of the Canadian Labatt group. Although its products are still confined very much to the northeastern region, Moretti produces one of Italy's most interesting ranges of beers: an excellent pilsner; a strong coppery beer (ABV 7.5 percent), la Rossa; the pure-malt, amber-coloured Baffo d'Oro; as well as a 'Double Brown'. Another popular beer is Prinz Bräu, owned for many years by the German Oetker group.

MALTA

Though independent, Malta has not thrown off all British influence, and beer drinkers will be pleasantly surprised to find some excellent top-fermentation ales produced by Simonds Farsons Cisk, the island's only brewery. As well as its own lager and the Carlsberg lager it brews under licence, Simonds produces a pale ale, Hopleaf; a mild, Blue Label; a sweetish stout, Lacto Milk; and a strong ale, Farsons. The malts and hops are imported from Britain. The company also accounts for most of the soft drinks consumed on the island (mainly Schweppes tonic waters and Pepsi).

GREECE

In Greece, as in other Mediterranean countries (Italy excepted), the amount of beer drunk has increased steadily over the years and the annual per capita figure now stands at 40 litres. Since the monopoly enjoyed by the national Fix group was terminated in 1960, foreign brewers have largely taken over the market (Fix itself went out of business in 1984). The predominant beers are premium lagers. A good example is Spartan, which is also exported to Greek restaurants in other countries.

The Heineken-owned Athenian Breweries account for 75 percent of total sales, their four plants producing mainly Heineken and Amstel beers. The other big group,

Henninger Hellas is, as the name suggests, of German origin (brand names Henninger, Kaiser and Germania), but was taken over in 1989 by the French BSN group, which now intends to introduce its Kronenbourg beers.

Löwenbräu withdrew in the 1980s, after an earlier period of activity, but has recently set up again under the name of Löwenbräu Hellas, complete with its own brewing installations. The remainder of the market consists of imported beers, the volume of which increased tenfold between 1982 and 1990.

Beer is sold mainly in Greece's tavernas and other restaurants, bars and pubs. Sales in shops and supermarkets are still very limited.

THE NEAR EAST

In the Muslim countries of the Mediterranean region beer is not officially approved of, though breweries exist or have existed in Iraq (Ferida, Golden, Jawhara), Iran (Shams, Medjidieh) and the Lebanon (Almaza).

Though Turkey has been secular in outlook since the time of Kemal Atatürk, its brewing industry is of fairly recent origin. The market leader, the Efes Pilsen Group, set up its first brewery in Istanbul in 1969, followed immediately by another at Izmir. It now also owns a third plant, at Adana, together with maltings at Afyon and Konya, in Anatolia, and has been producing its own hops since 1971.

Efes beers are for the most part conventional lagers, though the company also produces a darker, Munich-style beer, and an alcohol-free product. Given the large numbers of Turks resident in other parts of Europe, Efes beers are labelled in various languages (particularly German and Dutch).

Including Löwenbräu beer, which its brews under licence, the Efes group's production capacity is in excess of five million hectolitres.

Finally, Tuborg has been operating at Izmir since 1969, and there is another brewery at Ankara, whose beers bear the Tekel label.

In Israel, the main brewing concern is a subsidiary of the Canadian Labatt group. It produces a number of brews, including Maccabee, a kosher beer, which is also exported. To win the approval of the religious authorities, a kosher beer must be made from barley and hops cultivated in accordance with the precepts of the Mosaic law. In particular, the land on which they are grown must be left fallow at seven-year intervals, and brewing is forbidden during the Jewish Passover. As well as a number of pilsners (O.K., Abir, Nesher), the brewery produces an ale, Goldstar.

FORMER YUGOSLAVIA

The Southern Slav lands have a brewing tradition going back to the 13th century, and the region is renowned for both the quality of its hops and the purity of its spring waters. Before the country began to fall apart, there were thirty or so breweries in operation – no fewer than a century ago, when brewing underwent its industrial revolution.

Yugoslavia's membership of the Austro-Hungarian Empire was, not surprisingly, a major factor in the development of the industry. The Apatin brewery, for instance, was set up in 1756 with the patronage of the Imperial Chamber of Commerce in Vienna. Austrian influence is evident to this day in the way bottles are labelled, as breweries still use the Plato system to indicate the alcoholic strength of their products, in conjunction with the term 'extract'. A beer advertised as 'Extract 11.6 percent' would have an ABV rating of 5 percent.

Most of the beers currently produced are blond lagers, and come in bottles of 50 and 30 centilitres.

Protected from outside competition for many years, some breweries are of very

long standing. The oldest, located in the Croatian town of Osijek, in fact dates back to 1697.

Present-day Yugoslavia, which consists of Serbia and Montenegro, possesses thirteen different brewing companies, whose product is aimed almost exclusively at the local market. The biggest, founded in 1850, is based in Belgrade and produces over 1.2 million hectolitres a year. Its main brand is Gold Beer.

The oldest brewery in Serbia, dating from 1722, is at Pancevo. It brews 250,000 hectolitres a year of its Standard and, slightly stronger (ABV 5 percent+), Weifert brands.

Though founded in 1745, the Zrenjanin brewery has the most modern facilities in Serbia. It produces some highly regarded blond and brown beers, which are

packaged exclusively in half-litre bottles. The beers of the Trebjesa brewery at Niksic owe their quality to the spring water piped from the surrounding mountains. They have won several international awards over the years. Founded in 1896, the brewery has an annual production capacity of 750,000 hectolitres. Its leading brand is called Gold Beer Big Nik.

Featuring a stag on its labels, the Apatin brewery is also renowned for the quality of its beers. It produces 250,000 hectolitres a year, packaging its products in 50 and 30 centilitre bottles.

Water of the highest quality is again a factor in the success of the beers produced by the local brewery at Zajecar, close to the Bulgarian border. It was founded in 1895 and now produces nearly 500,000

hectolitres of beer a year.

The Nis brewery, founded in 1884, produces a beer which won a gold medal at Geneva in 1972. It has an annual production figure of around 600,000 hectolitres.

Also of interest is the brewery at Valjevo, which produces the German-sounding Eichinger brand. One of its beers is brewed from oats and barley malt.

The small Inex brewery at Vrsac (150,000 hectolitres per annum) makes a habit of winning international awards: its Champion brand took first prize in Luxembourg in 1979. This brewery is particularly ancient, dating from 1849.

THE NEW WORLD

The natives of the Americas were making fermented beverages from cereals long before the arrival of Christopher Columbus. Maize, staple of the Inca and Andean civilisations, was used in brewing the alcoholic drinks consumed at religious rituals and in the course of everyday life. In Amazonia, cassava served the same purpose. From those far-off days, only *chicha* remains, while beers of European derivation have conquered the entire continent, from Alaska to Tierra del Fuego.

Settlers and pioneers soon adopted the lager-type beers produced in Czechoslovakia and Germany as being the most satisfactory thirst-quenchers, and this led in North America to the creation of industrial giants, whose monopoly was further strengthened during the Prohibition era. Only in recent times has their domination been challenged, with a more demanding generation of consumers prevailing on brewers – on both the East Coast and in California – to come up with a greater variety of beers, many of them inspired by British ales.

Also based on German models, the beers of Latin America are seen mainly as an inexpensive way of laying the dust. Their exotic quality derives more often from the decorative label than from any originality in taste. In a throwback to pre-Columbian days, maize is often mixed with the barley, giving them more body than their North American counterparts.

Above: a Native American in a US bar.
Right: Preparing a brew based on wheat in pre-Columbian America, from an illustration by Théodore de Bry, a flemish explorer of the 16th century.

NORTH AMERICA

While clearly deriving from European models, over a time-span of almost two centuries the beers of North America have not surprisingly developed a culture of their own. Lager beers, originally of Czech and German inspiration, hog the limelight, produced in colossal factories by some of the world's biggest industrial enterprises. There is a touch of originality in the light versions of these beers and, more recently, in the 'dry' style of lager: rediscovery of the bitter taste of hops raises hopes that the American consumer is becoming more discerning. At the other end of the scale, artisan brewers have begun to emerge in the last ten years, and the British-style ales they are offering have met with considerable success. Sine qua non of a baseball final or an evening spent watching television, beer is also the mainstay of the ubiquitous American bar, whether a classy Washington rendezvous or an anonymous roadside halt in the Middle West.

It is quite amazing that, unlike Mickey Mouse, Coca-Cola or cowboy films, this pillar of American civilisation has found so little favour abroad. Whereas the Dutch with their Heineken, the Australians, and even the Mexicans, are making greater and greater inroads into export markets, it is still not easy to find an American beer outside its country of origin, despite the recent European investments of the colossus Anheuser-Busch.

Big and small, often animated by live music, bars in the United States are places where people go in search of company and to enjoy a few beers.

NORTH AMERICA

Beer, like many other aspects of life in the United States, tends to confirm the American reputation for doing things on a grand scale. The world's biggest producer of the beverage, the US holds records in every department: in 1991 the twelve breweries of the Anheuser-Busch group produced close on 110 million hectolitres – almost as much as the 1,200 German breweries put together! Brewed mainly for home consumption, only two percent of this total was exported, though 2.2 million hectolitres can hardly be described as small beer!

Beer found its way to the Americas with the early European immigrants. The Pilgrim Fathers recorded in the ship's log of the *Mayflower* a decision to land on the northeast coast, not further south as planned, because they were short of victuals, especially beer.

Like the English, the Germans soon began producing their favourite drink in the New World. The first recorded brewery was established in New Amsterdam (now New York) in 1623. George Washington operated his own brewery at Mount Vernon (though he was more interested in selling whisky); and at Monticello, the manuscript of Thomas Jefferson's recipe for beer – dated 1757 – is still carefully preserved.

Fresh waves of immigrants from Central Europe brought with them the know-how for brewing bottom-fermentation beers. Companies were set up to produce them, and their growth was encouraged by the development of the railways. The possibilities of this form of transport loomed large in the mind of a young

brewer, Adolphus Busch. In 1861 he married Lilly Anheuser, heiress of a brewer from Saint Louis, Missouri. (Anheuser senior had acquired the business in 1852, when Saint Louis was still a frontier town on the route west). Adolphus Busch decided to transport his beers in refrigerated vehicles and railroad wagons to ensure that they reached their destination in perfect condition. This system is still adhered to today, and followed by subsidiaries throughout the

world, including Europe and Asia: if a Parisian café proprietor is to serve Michelob, the group's premium beer, he must prove that he has his own cold store – and his wholesaler a refrigerated depot – to ensure that, down the whole distribution chain, the beer is kept at a temperature of 4°C.

After a century of continuous growth, Anheuser-Busch is still a family business (its present boss, August Busch III, representing the fourth generation, has presided over the group's fort-unes since 1974) and has remained faithful to its founder's principles in respect of quality. During the fermentation process its breweries still use a time-honoured method, now abandoned virtually everywhere in Europe: beech chippings are put into the coppers for the yeast to settle on, thereby ensuring better contact with the wort.

The group's three principal brands, Busch, Budweiser and Michelob, are available in a number of different versions: light, dark and dry. There is even an Anheuser Märzen Beer, proof that American brewers are mindful of their Central European origins, even though they operate on an altogether grander scale. Anheuser's biggest plant (on the site of the original brewery in Saint Louis, part of which is now classified as a historical monument) produces more beer than he whole of the Belgium industry. Jealous of its reputation, Anheuser-Busch puts a lot of money and effort into environmental programmes (first and foremost the

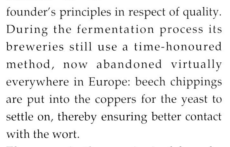

Adolphus Busch

recycling of empty cans), and subsidises efforts to com-bat alcoholism, especially among young people.

As it controls almost 45 percent of the American market, Anheuser-Busch is far larger than any of its rivals. They are Miller (part of the Philip Morris group), Coors, Stroh, Heileman (owned by Bond of Australia) and Pabst, in that order.

The Germanic origins of these companies, especially those implanted in the Middle West, is obvious – the Stroh family were from the Rhineland Palatinate; Jacob Pabst was born in Leipzig – and they have maintained some of the old techniques. The coppers of the Stroh breweries, for instance, are still direct-fired.

The Coors group, implanted at the foot of the Rocky Mountains, where the pure spring water is an excellent selling point, is also conservative in approach. Although Coors produces beer in vast quantities in its huge, ultra-modern plant (over 23 million hectolitres a year), its products are not pasteurised, but undergo a sterile filtration process.

The current concentration and gigantism of the American brewing industry derives in large part from the Prohibition era. Efforts to prevent the manufacture of alcohol led to the closure of hundreds of small and medium-sized breweries, which failed to find other channels for their manufacturing capacity. When

Prohibition was finally lifted and the authorities returned to a more reasonable policy, only the big operators had survived and were able to increase their influence. During this period, Anheuser-Busch had become the country's biggest producer of bakers' yeast, while Coors made malted milk drinks.

Competition then centred on light beers, which seem almost insipid to a European palate. Miller's Lite is an excellent example. But it was possible to go only so far down this road (though there has been a recent revival in interest), and the current fashion is for the more bitter 'dry' beers.

But the real feature of the 1980s was a cut-throat price war, which shook the market from top to bottom. Whereas the three biggest groups continued to expand and grow – Anheuser-Busch actually produced a phenomenal 110 hectolitres in 1992 (a tenth of total world production) – some of the smaller producers proved unequal to the struggle. Stroh, for instance, saw its production volumes decline by a third, and over a six-year period Heileman, the number five, experienced a fall-off in sales of 45 percent. Only Pabst, sixth in the national rankings, managed to more or less hold its own, though at the cost of a debilitating price-cutting policy.

Dogged by the constant threat of merger or takeover, these groups have reacted by introducing new brands of beer, often for regional distribution. In this respect, Heileman takes the laurels, having launched thirty or so new beers – or variants of existing beers – in the last ten years: Blitz Weinhardt, Rainer, Colt 45, Culmbacher Imperial Dark, and many

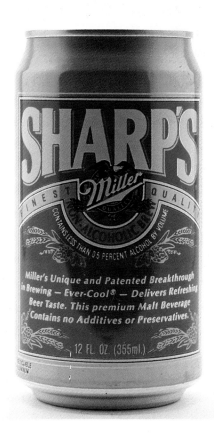

A TALE OF TWO BUDWEISERS

Two beers bearing the name Budweiser co-exist quite legally. The American version, masterpiece of the Anheuser-Busch group, is the world's most heavily sold beer. First brewed in 1876, this Budweiser takes its name from a Czech brewing town, Budweis (nowadays Ceské Budejovice), which in its day was as famous as Pilsen. When the American Budweiser came to such prominence, the Czech brewers took umbrage and argued that they alone should be entitled to use the name. The Czechs were producing a Budweiser Budvar, but the brewery concerned was not founded until 1895, so the American brand was able to claim seniority.

Czech influence is also evident in other beers produced by the Anheuser-Busch group: Michelob derives its name from another Czechoslovakian town and, during the Prohibition era, the group manufactured a malted drink known as Pivo, the Slav term for beer.

more. Their Germanic overtones are often more a question of packaging than of substance. Stroh, for its part, has introduced Signature, Schaefer and several versions of Old Milwaukee, to which Pabst has replied with Olympia, Ice Man, Old English and Hamm in various guises.

This policy has not always been crowned with success. Heileman even drew censure from the government when, in 1990, it launched Powermaster, a very strong malt beer targeted at ethnic minorities living in the big cities. The latent American puritanism in such matters soon forced the brewery to abandon its plans.

Because lagers of German and Czech derivation are so dominant in the United States, many Americans are not even aware of the existence of other types of beer. Locally, however, there is a growing interest in other varieties, particularly ales styled on the British model.

Writing in the early 1980s, the well known author Michael Jackson listed at least 300

American beers; and in the last 20 years over 100 micro-breweries, serving relatively small areas, have been set up on the East Coast, as well as in California and the central states.

Ale continues to be the preferred style of beer-drinkers in the northeast, though the local version differs quite considerably from its British originals: the beer is brewed at the higher temperatures required for an ale, but often without the authentic top-fermentation yeasts. America's seventh biggest brewer,

Geneese, operating from Rochester in the state of New York, produces only beers of this type, to the tune of 2.6 million hectolitres a year. It even includes a porter in its range.

Specific to the United States, cream ale was originally a blend of ale and lager. The term is now applied to sweetish beers of distinctly golden coloration. New Amsterdam Amber Ale, produced by the small Uttica brewery near New York, is another good example of an ale in the American style.

The Boston area, home to a number of flourishing micro-breweries, also boasts a fine golden lager, Samuel Adams, which combines great smoothness with a strong,

BROOKLYN, A BEER REVIVED

A perfect example of the renaissance of artisan brewing in the United States, Brooklyn Lager was born of the desire of two enthusiasts to find a beer exactly to their taste. The historic decision was taken in 1986, as they sat watching a baseball match on television. Obsessed with the idea, journalist Steve Hindy and banker Tom Potter eventually gave up their jobs to make their desire a reality. Taking advice from a retired brewer, they finally produced a beer of considerable character, combining malt with a strong, hoppy flavour. It is conditioned for between six and eight weeks before going on sale.

The name refers back to the good old days when New York could boast a good 40 breweries. Graced with a label by the great American designer Milton Glaser, Brooklyn Lager is already widely exported: more than 10 percent of the 15,000 litres produced annually finds its way abroad.

hoppy flavour. The name commemorates a hero of the War of Independence, by trade a brewer. This style goes down well in New England, where it has spawned a number of imitations, among them Harpoon.

Though a fairly conventional lager, Rolling Rock, produced at Latrobe in the vicinity of the Great Lakes, has sold well thanks to its transparent bottle and unusual label (reproduced by a silk-screen process). It is in demand abroad and also has its imitators: Gator and Snake beer, for example. The Mexican Corona beer may have been behind these developments: its bottle was the first of this kind to appear in the United States, and Corona was at first very competitively priced.

The State of New York, by the way, is still a great brewing region. There is even a brewery in Brooklyn, which features a 'pre-prohibition' beer.

Independent breweries are fewer in the

southern states, where the big national groups hold sway. New Orleans is nevertheless home to the firm of Dixie, a name redolent of the Old South, which produces a pleasant light beer of the same name. In Texas, Lone Star, well-hopped for an American beer, claims to be 'the beer of the Texan nation', even though it belongs to the Heileman group! There are several other breweries in the state.

As well as supporting a large number of micro-breweries, California is the birthplace of one of the American continent's few truly original brews: Anchor Steam Beer. This product is the result of a technical compromise, arrived at in the last century, when the colonisation of the state was in full swing. American immigrants were arriving with new techniques and yeasts suitable for the bottom fermentation process. But the local breweries, lacking sufficient quantities of ice, were unable to cool the fermenting worts to the proper temperature. They therefore adopted the technique of brewing at temperatures suitable for top fermentation, but in shallow mash tuns. The beer thus obtained is extremely frothy and, when served on draught, produces a characteristic hissing sound, which earned it the nickname of steam beer.

This type of beer all but disappeared in 1965, when San Francisco's last surviving brewery seemed likely to close. It was saved at the eleventh hour by Fritz Maytag, scion of a family of wealthy industrialists, who has considerably developed the brewery in recent years. As well as the well-hopped steam beer, he has created or revived other styles, for instance the more potent Liberty Ale.

In the Western states, the most interesting beers are as a rule produced by micro-

investments in other countries. Carling is the lager now distributed in large quantities by Bass in Britain.

breweries and can be had only on the premises. Exceptions are the many – very British – beers brewed by the Grant brewery in Washington state, in the heart of the hop-growing region.

In Canada, the industry is organised on similar lines: three large companies have taken the lion's share of the market, while micro-breweries thrive on the fringes. The big difference is that – due to British influence – the major brewing groups also produce top-fermentation ales, though there are plenty of lagers to choose from.

Founded in 1782 by an Englishman, Molson still belongs to the same family, making it North America's oldest surviving brewery. More than any other, it has remained faithful to the British style of beer, and also produces a porter.

Labatt, Canada's biggest brewing concern, concentrates on lagers. Canadian lagers are more rugged in character than their US counterparts, and for this reason people wrongly think of them as stronger. The company belongs to a branch of the Bronfman family, which also controls the Seagram group, the world's biggest producer of wines and spirits.

Canada's third biggest brewer, Carling O'Keefe, is now owned by the Australian Elders group. Like its fellow-Australian rival, Bond, Elders is one of the few brewing concerns to have made massive

LATIN AMERICA

The Spanish and Portuguese *conquistadores* had little in the way of beer to ship with them to the New World, and it was only at a much later stage that pilsners of Czech and German inspiration began to supersede the traditional maize or cassava-based beers of South America. There is something incongruous in drinking a Bohemia beer in Mexico or asking for a Munich beer in Venezuela, but there is no denying the influence of the Old World.

As in Africa, the rather pale South American beer – served chilled or even iced – is a basic, unpretentious drink, differing little from one country to another. There are, fortunately, some interesting exceptions, such as the strong beers of the Caribbean, or *malta*, a strange, alcohol-free drink made with malt extract, which has at least the taste of the real McCoy. But the Mexican phenomenon proves that things can develop with unexpected rapidity. Following in the footsteps of Corona (now the tenth most popular beer in the world), Mexican brands began to make an impact on the United States because they were competitively priced. Subsequently they became an object of curiosity, particularly in Europe, where, like tequila, they have an aura of tropical exoticism.

Left: a bar in Cuba. Widely drunk throughout Latin America, beer has become increasingly popular in the last few years. Its expansion is aptly symbolised by this giant bottle (above), on display in Chile.

LATIN AMERICA

Among the Incas living around Lake Titicaca, it was the task of hand-picked young maidens to chew the cooked maize pulp used in making beer: only their saliva – it was believed – would cause the sacred beverage to ferment. Needless to say, these production methods did not survive the Spanish and Portuguese colonisations, though *chica*, a traditional maize beer, is still brewed in the high plateau country of the Andes, and cassava beers can still be found in Amazonia.

Some years ago an American enthusiast, Alan Eames (nicknamed the Indiana Jones of beer), had the bright idea of reviving extinct beverages. One of his obsessions was the 'black beer' once brewed in Amazonia from dark-roasted barley and maize. It was flavoured with lupins and left to ferment by the action of wild yeasts. In the more distant past

cassava was also used as an ingredient. By dint of much travelling and research Eames eventually rediscovered the recipe and, though cassava (which can be toxic) was excluded, managed to brew his own black beer. He called it Xingu, the name of the Amazon tributary on whose banks live the last surviving Indian tribes of the region. Xingu has found a ready market in the Boston area of the United States.

Dark beers, browns and stouts, are well represented in Latin America, particularly in the Caribbean. For instance, the brown Porter 39, hailing originally from northern France, has been a great hit in Guadeloupe and Martinique, while Guinness has found a profitable market in Jamaica and throughout the West Indies for a stout of greater potency than its Irish original. It would appear that beers of this type have

aphrodisiac qualities – a good selling point in these exotic climes.

More conventional lagers are also produced in large quantities in the West Indies, with many of the breweries controlled by international giants such as Heineken. The Dutch group has a stake in the Red Stripe brewery, which produces Jamaica's most popular beer. It is even exported to the United States, and in Britain is brewed under licence. As its label proclaims, Red Stripe is brewed at

low temperatures, which gives it a good nose. Typical of the smaller, rather old-fashioned breweries of the region is that of the Turks and Caicos Islands.

We have already mentioned *malta*, a very popular beverage in the Caribbean. It is not so much an alcohol-free beer as a soft drink made from malt extract.

Mexico has a well-developed brewing industry. The strong Central European influence of the early days is still evident in its Bohemia brand, an amber-coloured, well-hopped beer (ABV 4.8 percent) claiming Czech antecedents. Some of the hops that go into it are still in fact imported from the Czech Republic.

Three groups operating a dozen or so breweries account for the bulk of Mexico's beer production. The brand that has made Mexican beer popular abroad is Corona, typical of the thirst quenchers enjoyed by the working classes. Served in a transparent bottle with a round of lemon, it is all the rage in 'Tex-Mex' restaurants throughout the States and is currently gearing up to conquer Europe, where the fashion for Mexican cookery and tequila is also gaining ground. In Spain, where the

Corona trade mark is already used for a range of wines, the Mexican beer is sold as Coronita. In Germany it has even inspired an imitation.

Another lager packaged in a transparent bottle is the very similar Sol, produced by the Moctezuma group. Moctezuma also markets Dos Equis, a well-balanced, golden-coloured beer in the Munich style. An amber version is also available.

Another popular lager-type beer is Tecate, often drunk, like tequila, with salt and a slice of lime. Other popular Mexican brands are the easily digested Superior, and Carta Blanca, one of the country's oldest beers.

Throughout South America beer is an everyday drink catering to an expanding market, but the local products are as yet unknown in Europe. In Brazil, for instance, there are three major brewers: Brahma of Rio de Janeiro (which owns a score of breweries), the Sao Paulo-based Antarctica Paulista,

and Skol-Caracu, linked with the Canadian Labatt group. Brahma and Antarctica rank among the world's top twenty: in 1991 Brahma in fact produced over 31 million hectolitres. Its range includes Brahma Chopp and other lagers, and even a top-fermentation porter with an ABV rating of over 8 percent.

In Venezuela, Polar lager, brewed by the Polar company, is the world's ninth-ranking brand in volume terms: over 12 million hectolitres produced in 1991. The name might (or might not) seem strange in these latitudes, accentuated as it is by the cool blue and white of the

label. Another Venezuelan group, Cardenal, produces both European-style lagers such as Munich and Nacional (advertised as a pilsner) and Andes, a beer of more obvious South American flavour, brewed mainly for export.

According to the American magazine *Impact*, the Columbian brewer Santo Domingo, producer of the Aguila brand, this year achieved seventeenth place in the world rankings, a position that many European brewers might envy: of the Europeans, only Heineken, the French BSN group, Carlsberg and Bass actually figure in the top twenty.

South American beers are most commonly packaged in bottles of 60 centilitres and over. For this reason, 33-centilitre cans are synonymous with

higher quality and are relatively more expensive.

On the whole, though, beer remains an unpretentious, everyday drink to which no one pays much attention, on a par with the ubiquitous international lagers. Though slightly denser and fuller-bodied than their North American counterparts, Latin American beers generally lack distinguishing characteristics; hence the Germanic borrowings, which may even include gothic characters on the label. For

the brewing operation, maize is often used in conjunction with barley, but this link with the old pre-Columbian beers is only of nominal interest: modern manufacturing processes are such that there is precious little evidence of it in the taste of the end product.

It is nevertheless to be hoped that the rapid rise of Mexican Corona (whose export volumes have increased 170-fold in the last ten years) and the fascination exercised by Latin America generally will

provide the brewers of this region with the means to expand and develop new products. Given the production volumes being achieved by Mexico, Brazil, Venezuela and Chile, it is almost certain that we shall be hearing more of their beers in years to come.

ASIA

For thousands of years the Chinese, Japanese and other Asian peoples have made fermented beverages from their staple cereals – millet, rice, sorghum and wheat – though the results are often more akin to spirits than to barley-based beers. Some of these are still produced, but during the last hundred years beers brewed from malt and hops on European lines have come to the fore throughout the area. In Australia and New Zealand, British ales were introduced by the early settlers, to be followed in due course by American lagers.

Pale pilsners in China, high-tech lagers in Japan stouts derived from the ever-present Guinness in Southern Asia: the tastes of Asian beers are a good deal less surprising than their packaging. Exotic labels featuring dragons and cherry trees in flower provide a fascinating spectacle in themselves. The big European brewers (Heineken, Carlsberg, Kronenbourg, BGI), and of course the Australians, are also very active in a market where the real competitor is not wine – an expensive luxury – but soft drinks, starting with the ubiquitous Coca-Cola. The success of Oriental restaurants in Europe should put European brewers on their guard: beer is an excellent accompaniment to the dishes they serve, and they form an ideal bridgehead for Asian brewers wanting to gain a toehold in the West. An eventual swing of the commercial pendulum would come as no surprise.

Above: Quingdao (or Tsing Tao), China's best-known export beer, is considered a luxury on the home market.
Left: as in this crowded Hong Kong restaurant, mild, low-alcohol beers are a fitting accompaniment to Asian cuisine.

CHINA

During the four thousand years of its existence, subjects of the Middle Empire have produced a number of fermented drinks made from cereals: *tsiou* (or *shu*), brewed from millet; *chiu* made from wheat; then various rice-based beverages (for instance, *p'ei*, meaning 'floating ants' on account of the debris likely to rise to the surface). Were these really beers in the modern sense of the term? It is true that these drinks were produced by steeping the grain and fermenting the resulting liquid rather than by distillation. And yet, it is difficult to accept that almost colourless beverages without a head – like the Japanese sake – deserve to be called beers. It is interesting to note that one of Marco Polo's companions refers to them as *vinum de riso*, 'rice wine', rather than as beer.

There is in any case no record of beverages having been brewed from malted barley, though hops would seem to have been used as early as the 18th century. This coincides with the establishment of the early European trading posts, particularly the German settlement in the port of Tsing Tao on the China Sea, facing Japan and South Korea. Faithful to their customs, the Germans soon set up a brewery to produce a pilsner to their taste. The Tsing Tao brand exists to this day and is exported to many parts of the world, in both bottles and cans.

According to Marc Boulet, in China itself Tsing Tao beer is expensive and hard to find, but beer is in any case something of a luxury, costing almost as much as spirits. He believes there to be over five hundred brands of beer in China, produced by a large number of provincial breweries, such as Huiquan, Bandao or Cuidao. However, they lack originality, most of them being pale lagers with little flavour or body.

Beijing, the beer of Peking, is a more aromatic product. For many years it was the official drink offered at Communist Party banquets, out of the reach of ordinary mortals.

Michael Jackson also mentions some non-lager beers – sweet, cloudy brews akin to ales, for instance the Wei Mei and Mon Lei brands from Peking – and Guangminpai, a dark lager from Shanghai. But none of these is exported. The only Chinese beers available in Europe are in fact the Tsing Tao brand and a few lagers of similar type.

JAPAN

Although sake, the traditional 'rice beer', is still the most popular alcoholic beverage consumed in the Land of the Rising Sun, European-style beers have been gaining ground over the last hundred years. Long protected by solid customs barriers, the Japanese brewing industry is nowadays one of the most powerful and dynamic in all Asia.

When, in 1869, Japan at last opened its doors to foreign trade, the first brewery was set up at Yokohama by an American, William Copeland, to meet the needs of foreign residents. It eventually passed into Japanese ownership as the Kirin brewery, and a beer of that name continues to be one of the most popular national brands.

Wanting to learn to brew barley beers, the Japanese looked first to Germany, sending an official mission to that country in 1870.

Subsequently, in 1876, the first national brewery was established on the northern island of Hokkaido: the Sapporo brewery was born.

The Japanese brewing industry is dominated by lagers, which are extremely light and clean-tasting, though not without body. As in the United States, the more bitter 'dry' style has come to the fore in recent years: it was launched by Asahi in 1987 and has since been imitated by the other brewers.

The first German-style brasserie was opened in 1899 in the Ginza (the fashionable quarter of Tokyo). Nowadays, a great deal of beer is drunk in delightful 'gardens' of ornamental trees and pot

plants located on the top storey of high buildings.

The Japanese brewing industry is in the hands of six major groups – Sapporo, Asahi, Kirin, Hokkaido Asahi, Orion and Suntory – who together operate some forty breweries. Suntory, the country's biggest producer of wines and spirits, did not become involved in beer until 1963: the fact that the group now owns three big plants indicates how strongly the Japanese market has continued to expand. The brewers are not immune to the Japanese passion for anything high-tech, and in recent years they have invested heavily in ways of improving their production methods. Sapporo, a company proud to have had an R&D budget since the turn of the century, has introduced an exclusive, state-of-the-art process of ceramic micro-filtering. The resulting beer is completely free of residual yeasts, which gives it a cleanest-of-clean taste and obviates the need for pasteurisation. Sapporo has also revolutionised packaging, introducing a new-shape metal can for its Silver brand. It sits nicely in the hand, and keeps the beer cool longer than more conventional containers. It has met with considerable success, in both Europe and the United States.

Japanese brewers offer a quite extensive range of beers, available in bottles, cans and mini-kegs. Besides its standard Draft brand, Sapporo markets a 'dry'; a top of the range pure malt beer, Yebisu; a well-hopped brown reminiscent of American malt liquors, Black Beer; and a richly-structured Christmas beer, Winter's Tale. Its more recent Baisen Draft, brewed from a combination of light and dark malts, is of a transparent brown colour, sweetish in taste and pleasantly aromatic.

Fifth in the world rankings, the Kirin group derives its name, and label, from a mythical Chinese animal, half-horse, half-dragon, believed to bring good luck. Kirin's pilsners are closely modelled on German originals: one is even called Mein Bräu! The range also includes a brown Black Beer in the Bavarian style, and a strong stout (ABV 8 percent). The company controls a dozen or so breweries throughout the archipelago.

When Suntory defined its range of beers some thirty years ago, it drew inspiration from the fresh, clean taste of Danish lagers of the Carlsberg type, which accord well with traditional Japanese cooking. Fervent advocates of biological testing, the Suntory technicians have also opted for micro-filtration, to avoid the need for pasteurising their beers. Apart from its basic lager, the company markets Malt's, which, as its name suggests, has a distinctly malty flavour, and, more recently, Ginjo, a much sweeter product. Since 1989, Suntory has operated its own micro-brewery, conducting regular experiments with new types of beer.

The Japanese brewers all produce a number of international brands under licence: Budweiser and Carlsberg in the case of Suntory; Guinness and Miller in the case of Sapporo.

THE FAR EAST

Many other Asian countries have brewing industries of some importance, often marked by their colonial heritage. Such is the case in Vietnam, where French brewers once held sway. Now that the country again has links with the non-communist world, the Vietnamese government has, not surprisingly, called on the French BGI company (Brasseries et glacières internationales, part of the Castel group) to build a new brewing plant at My Tho, in the south of the country. It should come on stream in the course of 1993, helping to make up the current shortfall in production. BGI was a fitting choice, since the group was born in Indochina, in 1875, and its '33' brand has always been virtually synonymous with the word beer.

In Thailand, the Boon Rawd brewery's Singha brand was first produced in the 1930s, in imitation of strong, well-hopped German lagers. The export version has an ABV rating of 6 percent. Other lagers brewed in Thailand are the Kloster and Thai Amarit brands.

Singapore may well have been

independent of the Federation of Malaysia for the last twenty-five years, but its Tiger lager continues to form a bridge between the two countries: it is produced in both Kuala Lumpur and Singapore, where the dynamic brewery operates in association with Heineken. The island's other main brand is Anchor,

while a creamy, caramel-flavoured stout is brewed by the Archipelago Brewery Company (ABC). Stouts are much appreciated in many parts of Southern Asia, where Guinness has enjoyed a solid reputation for over a century.

In the Philippines, the market is largely controlled by the San Miguel group, which operates four breweries. Established in 1890 as a subsidiary of a Spanish brewing enterprise, San Miguel eventually became independent but has

retained its original name. Its main brand is a lager, Pale Pilsen, whose label is applied by the silk-screen process. This beer also comes in 'dry' and brown (Cerveza Negra) versions. Other San Miguel products are the stronger, blond Red Horse, and Gold Eagle. The company is also into soft drinks. Highly dynamic, San Miguel has recently set up a brewery in China, in partnership with the authorities at Guangzou, and has interests in Vietnam and Hong Kong.

In the Indian sub-continent, British influence lingers on in the large number of stouts, widely available in the south and in Sri Lanka, where, as in the best Irish pubs, some are pumped by hand.

In Pakistan, the Murree brewery at Rawalpindi is well known for its London lager, though this is something of a misnomer. Lagers in fact form the bulk of the beer issuing from India's thirty or so breweries, the biggest of which are Mohan Meakin and United. In India, brewers have to contend with a diversity of laws, with some States all but prohibiting the manufacture and consumption of alcoholic beverages.

There are very few countries with no interest in beer. Nepal produces Star and Burma has its own Mandalay brand. Even Muslim countries are not entirely dry: beer is brewed in Iraq, and there were breweries in Iran until the advent of the ayatollahs.

AUSTRALIA

AND NEW ZEALAND

Above: Australians are among the greatest drinkers on the planet, as this manly ritual demonstrates! Right: they like their beer served cold, preferably in a can.

Well up in the top ten for beer consumption, Australia and New Zealand have also made a considerable impact on foreign markets, the ambitious Australian brewers having acquired businesses in the United States, Canada and Britain.

Australia's first known brewery was set up in Sydney in 1794 by a certain John Boston, who produced a fermented drink from maize and gooseberries! A century later, this vast country was served by over a score of breweries, and bottom-fermentation lagers soon began to supplant the ales and stouts preferred by the early British settlers.

Despite a long tradition of independent brewing, a series of takeovers and mergers in the last ten years has led to the formation of two main rival groups: Elders, whose leading brand is Foster's, and Bond, which brews Swan.

Although Australia is in some ways a conservative and rather puritan society, with opening hours even more complicated than Britain's and many restaurants not licensed to serve wine, a great deal of beer is drunk. Even so, the local market is not big enough for the two rival groups: a population of little over 17 million offers scant hope of expansion.

Contrary to usual practice, whereby penetration of foreign markets is achieved by brewing under licence rather then by

large-scale capital investment, in the 1980s the Australian brewers were the protagonists of some spectacular takeovers: Elders bought up Courage, one of the major British brewers, as a bridgehead for future expansion in Europe. They then acquired Carling, one of the biggest Canadian groups. Elders has recently put all its eggs in the brewing basket, selling other interests in the agri-foodstuffs sector. Meanwhile, Alan Bond, an enterprising businessman with a high media profile, had set his sights on Heileman, the fifth-ranking American brewer.

In Australia itself, Foster's lager has been around for over a century, named after two brothers who, due to their ownership of a refrigeration system, were the first to brew bottom-fermentation beers on the island. Now available in cans and bottles, Foster's, like most Australian lagers, is drunk very cold. Though it achieved full national coverage only recently, Foster's is already popular in many parts of the world.

The Elders group also markets a large number of other Australian brands. This is not surprising, since the present company resulted from the merger of several brewing concerns (one of its subsidiaries is called Carlton and Union Breweries). Most of its products are lagers: Carlton Crown, Abbots, and the

inappropriately named Victoria Bitter and Melbourne Bitter, which have nothing in common with British ales. The group also produces stouts, one rejoicing in the unusual name of Invalid!

Although in the eyes of the rest of the world the crocodile has been emblematic of Australia since the release of the film *Crocodile Dundee*, the animal which more than any other epitomises beer is the swan, its effigy gracing all the beers produced by the Bond group's Perth brewery. This lager comes in a good half-dozen versions, including the 0.9 percent ABV Special Light. Eligible for the European category of alcohol-free beers, this product was to have been brewed for the European market by the Belgian Interbrew group, until Bond decided to undertake the operation on its own account. The Swan range also includes a stout.

The black swan is not the Bond group's only trademark. Bond also markets the Emu range of lagers and the Queensland-based Castlemaine, whose XXXX symbol recalls the days when beer barrels were marked in this way with a hot iron. Castlemaine also produces a Gold Lager of higher alcohol content than the general run of Australian beers (which rarely exceed 4.5 percent ABV) and Carbine

stout, the only remaining vestige of a once flourishing trade.

Sydney, the great metropolis of the south, has a predilection – rare in Australia – for strong, amber-coloured beers, not unlike British ales. Some good examples are Tooheys Hunter Old, the Bond group's Tall Ship, and Elders' Kent Old Brown (formerly Tooth's Old).

The island of Tasmania, Australia's main hop and barley producing region, still boasts its own independent brewery, Cascade, founded in 1824. It produces an extensive range of bottom-fermentation beers – lagers, stouts and ales – although these styles do not always conform to their original models. The island's other brewery, Boag, is a subsidiary of Cascade. The town of Adelaide also has an independent brewery, Cooper's, founded in 1862, which is still in the hands of the original family. As well as producing conventional lagers, it has continued to brew top-fermentation ales in the great British tradition, which are aged in oak casks. At one time in danger of closure, the brewery has since been able to expand, a sign that Australians are beginning to appreciate beers other than

lagers. This trend is confirmed by the recent appearance of pub-breweries – described by Michael Jackson in his book – which are specialising in more original styles and flavours.

The navigator James Cook, who discovered New Zealand in the 18th century, was himself an amateur brewer: during one of his voyages he concocted a beverage from fermented molasses flavoured with pine resin and tea. The recipe has been lost, but the country's brewing industry has continued in fine style, even though it has recently crystallised around the big New Zealand Breweries and Dominion Breweries groups.

NZB's prime brand is the widely-exported Steinlager, which has won several international awards in recognition of its cleanness of taste. The group operates breweries in Auckland, Hastings and Christchurch. Its brands also include Rheineck, Leopard and Lion. Although brewed by bottom fermentation, the two Lion beers have a rougher, more malty flavour, reminiscent of ales.

AFRICA

Africa has always had its fermented beverages, made from different varieties of millet, generally brewed by the womenfolk in rural areas. It is a pity that these traditional brews have been forced to give way to bottom-fermentation pilsners, introduced to the towns by the European colonists, and that there has been no process of cross-fertilisation. A millet beer flavoured with bitter African herbs and brewed using modern technology to ensure quality and consistency would have been an interesting proposition. In a continent plagued with economic problems, the increasing cost of importing the raw materials for brewing European-style pilsners may perhaps persuade some brewers to try this idea, and at the same time rediscover their African roots. Whether or not this dream ever becomes reality, the fact remains that beer – traditional or imported – is the most popular drink enjoyed by Africans. Soft drinks are the only serious rivals to the beers available (light, or dark after the manner of a strong Irish stout). With wines and spirits unknown or beyond the reach of the majority, beer is a fundamental element in any African celebration.

Bottom-fermentation lagers of European extraction have captured the market in most African countries, as is evident in these photographs from Zaire.

AFRICA

In the marketplaces of West Africa, particularly in Burkina-Faso, it is not unusual to come across women selling *dolo*, a traditional drink made from millet. Always brewed by the womenfolk, who organise their activities on collective lines, *dolo* results from spontaneous fermentation and is flavoured with bitter herbs. The drink, which is also brewed for festivals, must be consumed within forty-eight hours.

Dolo is not the only fermented drink. In equatorial Africa, similar beverages are made from green bananas. They are always brewed by the women, and will only keep for short periods.

Sadly, their place is steadily being usurped by lager beers on the European pattern, first introduced by the colonists, which have since become the most popular drink in urban areas. The first

brewery in Zaire was set up in 1902 by the Jesuits of Ki-Santu.

The two main producers of European-style beers are the Republic of South Africa and Nigeria, the most populous countries on the African continent. Nigeria has some thirty breweries, most of them established in fairly recent times. The biggest is the locally-owned Golden Guinea Breweries, but international concerns are also represented: Heineken has a stake in Nigerian Breweries, and the French Castel and German Henninger groups are also present. Heineken in fact has interests in many parts of Africa, notably in Zaire, Rwanda, Burundi, the Congo, Ghana, Morocco and Angola.

Africa's biggest manufacturer of beer is currently the French Castel group, known back home as a specialist in wines and mineral waters. Castel has recently added greatly to its African empire by acquiring BGI (Brasseries et glacières internationales). Founded over a century ago in what was Tonkin (Indochina), this company achieved a position of strength in France's African colonies, a situation which continued after independence. For many years a subsidiary of Française de brasserie, BGI was eventually resold to Castel by Heineken, after the Dutch group had acquired the French mother company.

BGI currently produce 10 million hectolitres of beer and fizzy drinks a year. They control twenty-five breweries in fourteen countries – most of them in francophone Africa: Cameroon, Gabon, Nigeria, Niger, Burkina-Faso, Benin, Ivory Coast, Senegal, Mali, the Central African Republic, Zaire and Tunisia – together with a number of soft drinks factories, mineral-water bottling plants and glassworks. The company's main brands are '33' Export, Flag, Beaufort, Castel Beer, Regag and La Gazelle, but some simply bear the name of the brewery of origin. The most widely used container remains the 66-centilitre bottle, but 33 and even 25-centilitre forms are beginning to make their appearance. BGI also brew certain beers under licence, notably Guinness, Tuborg, Carlsberg, Mutzig and Amstel. In 1991, the company acquired from Heineken Cameroon's second largest brewery (International Brasserie), and in 1992 took advantage of privatisation in Benin to purchase La Béninoise.

The Carlsberg group's only direct African involvement is in Malawi, where it controls a brewery and a major drinks wholesaler, but its beers are also widely distributed in other countries.

The Belgian Interbrew group owns three breweries. In Zaire, Brasimba, founded in 1923, brews around a million hectolitres of its Simba and Tembo brands. In the Ivory Coast, Solibra, set up in 1960, produces three beers: Bock, Brune and Mamba, with a total annual volume of 1.3 million hectolitres. Mamba is exported to the United States. Finally, in the Central African Republic, Mocaf, a subsidiary of the French Armentières brewery until absorbed by Interbrew, has two brands to its name: Mocaf Blonde and Super Mocaf.

Most African breweries have an on-going problem of supply, barley in particular being hard to grow in local conditions. The bulk of the raw materials therefore have to be imported from Europe, and this inevitably leads to financial complications since the price of the finished product does not cover the cost of production. Nigeria has tried to force brewers to make use of local cereals: in 1965, these were to cover at least 25 percent of total supply, with a target of 100 percent by the 1990s. But the brewers argued that this constraint would make it impossible to produce the kind of lagers to which consumers were accustomed, such as Gulder, the local cereals being too low in fermentable starch.

Although lagers account for the bulk of production, stouts – local imitations of Guinness – remain popular, particularly in English-speaking countries. They are considerably stronger than their European counterparts, often with an ABV rating as high as 8 percent.

In Kenya, at higher altitudes, it is easier to grow barley and hops, which may explain why Kenya Breweries offer a wider range of beers than any available elsewhere in Africa. It includes Tusker lager, featuring an elephant on the label, a premium version of which is exported to the United States; Pilsner Lager; and the more aromatic White Cap, of which there is also an export version.

In the Republic of South Africa and Zimbabwe, where white dominance has been more prolonged, two types of beer have managed to co-exist, with lager beers more or less reserved for Whites

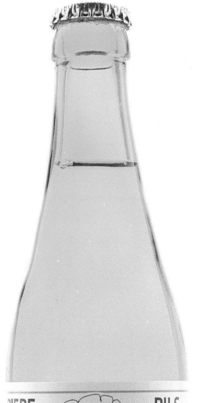

and the local 'kaffir' beer for the Blacks. The latter is one of the few traditional brews to have kept up with the times: made from sorghum, it is now brewed and produced on an industrial scale. In *l'Amateur de la bière*, Christian Berger reports that in Zimbabwe's second city of Bulawayo alone production of kaffir beer is of the order of 700,000 hectolitres a year. It was consumed mainly in beer gardens reserved for Blacks, consisting of an open-air area with a few benches.

Will the abolition of apartheid bring this curious situation to an end? Whatever happens, South Africa will remain a major beer producer. The two big brewing concerns in that country are South African Breweries, famous for Castle Lager and Lion Ale, and Intercontinental Breweries, which is owned by the Rothmans group. British and American influence in South Africa is such that already micro-breweries have begun to spring up, particularly in Cape Town.

In Madagascar, the sole brewing concern, STAR (Société tananarivienne de réfrigération), formerly affiliated to a French group, owns three breweries (at Antsirabe, Tulear and Diego Suarez) but normally produces just one brand, Three Horses Beer, or THB. The name is that of a brewery located at Breda in the Netherlands, but no one really knows how it came to be taken up in Madagascar. A lighter beer, Beek's Brau, is also sometimes available, and for special occasions the STAR has been known to produce a celebratory brew, for instance the anniversary Independence Beer, ABV 6.5 percent

THE COLONIAL ORIGINS OF '33' EXPORT

Contrary to popular opinion, the name of the French beer '33' Export does not derive from the former address of the Union de brasseries group, whose head office was for many years at 33 Avenue de Wagram in Paris, but from its colonial past. In the 1950s, BGI were generally marketing their beers in 65-centilitre bottles. Then stronger, more expensive European beers began to arrive, packaged in 33-centilitre containers. As a result, consumers would ask either for a 'normal' beer, or for a '33'. Anxious to keep up with demand and preserve their own market share, BGI responded by launching a pilsner known simply as '33' Export. Not until 1960 was this brand produced in France itself, where it quickly became one of the market leaders, particularly as a result of supermarket sales.

THE ART OF BEER DRINKING

Having considered the different styles of beer and the hundreds of brands produced all round the world, we now turn our attention to the specific language associated with beer, the way it should be drunk, and its use in cookery. Too many beer drinkers are unadventurous; content with a bland half pint in their local pub, when there is a vast range of different tastes to explore.

If they are to be appreciated as they deserve, beers must be kept and served with care. Most importantly, they should be drunk at the right temperature: no one would dream of serving a fine claret at 7°C; beer should be treated with just the same sort of respect. It is interesting that now, after years of neglect, some of the greatest French chefs are beginning to experiment with beer to enhance the flavour of their dishes – a new departure, promising some delightful surprises.

Over thousands of years, beer has generated a language and culture all of its own. This is the theme of psychologist Luce Janin-Devillars in the article that follows.

The complex tastes of the world's many styles and brands of beer are nowadays the subject of rigorous scientific study .

TALKING BEER:
IT'S A MAN'S WORLD

Although from early times beer was very much the preserve of women – in ancient Egypt, those involved in the brewing of fermented drinks came under the protection of Isis, goddess of the barley harvest – it is men who, over the years, have given the beverage its specific idiom and vocabulary.

'Due to our changeable climate and the need for social intercourse' wrote one commentator 'the brewery has become the equivalent of the forum of ancient times and the communal stove of the Middle Ages. There the menfolk meet to relax, to talk over public affairs and – let's be frank – to gossip'.

Gossip – there's a word to tickle the ears, and lead us, in the wake of the beer drinker, into the realm of … poetry!

The fact is that, between the silence of the teetotaller and that of the drinker whom alcohol has rendered insensible, there are two modes of speech, which reflect two approaches to beer (as there are two approaches to women): that of the connoisseur, who wishes to share his admiration and pleasure, and that of the consumer, whose conversation is limited to the number of pints he can drink.

We are, of course, more interested in the former. The connoisseur maintains with his favourite drink a relationship constantly sustained by observations from other areas of his experience. In writing of sauerkraut, for instance, the sociologist Julien Freud remarks that: 'It will tolerate red wine, has a weakness for beer, and is definitely flattered by white wine'.

Some beers, unfortunately, do not lend themselves to this sort of dialogue. They remain irritatingly dumb, stubbornly silent. They lack eloquence. A good beer, on the other hand, has the gift of the gab, provoking stimulating conversation.

Like many other things, beer has a secret inner life, but it is something of a mystery, not easily communicated in words. It needs to be sipped slowly at first, to let the palate take stock of its sweetness or pungency, drawing comparisons with soft fruits, lemon, apple or banana, even coffee.

Nor should the seeker fear to be seen with froth bejewelling his lips and moustache (an object of distaste to the uninitiated, as if the drinker were afflicted with some strange disease!). The drinker's enchanted look says it all: this is the object of my love.

Once the liquid has penetrated the inner man, where a sensation of coolness is quickly followed by one of warmth, its most intimate secrets are revealed.

Even so, the richness of sensations experienced by the drinker are never easily expressed in ordinary language. He must have recourse to poetry, to metaphor, to analogy, which may communicate his pleasure in striking images or fall ridiculously flat. The Germans, who have a wholehearted approach to the matter, call the head their 'pretty flower'. If the flower is satisfactory, claim the brewers, each sip will leave the drinker with a mouthful of 'Brussels lace'.

A good beer has first to be appreciated through the nose: its bouquet may be redolent of hops, flowers or herbs; some beers have a fragrance of spices or grilled meats. The connoisseur will note that a beer is 'light' in 'body', but not 'thin', or that it has a 'touch' of malt. Colours are expressed in terms of women's hair: one brew is 'fair', another 'blond', a third 'radiant'. Some beers are 'opaque with ebony highlights'; or they may be 'earth-coloured', 'autumnal', or 'brown, tending to reddish or mahogany'.

But drinkers do not always go in for such delicate flights of fancy. They are generally more down to earth: 'When you drink a few beers, you don't take them home with you. You pee them away at the pub!' Some of the good people of Munich will remember that, in their parents' day, the best beer cellars had drainage channels running beneath the tables, into which customers could relieve themselves without leaving their places or, of course, their glasses.

Those days may have gone for ever, but a pub, bar or beer cellar is still a microcosm of male society, a man's world, where tongues are loosened as quickly as neckties. Woman is not banned, but she must melt into the prevailing atmosphere – loosen her stays, as a man rolls up his sleeves. Licence is given that would cause offence in other circumstances: coarse language and crude gestures are tacitly permitted. Racy stories and spicy anecdotes are the order of the day.

A forbidden pleasure

Here, men freely enjoy a measure of that 'licence' generally frowned on by civilised society and the guardians of morality. Whereas convention and good manners demand moderation in speech and demeanour, here it is permitted to raise one's voice and use bad language. It is no secret that the crudest jokes are often the best. Casting off restraint and speaking freely of sex and excrement, one is putting oneself in the shoes of the child, who has not yet learned that such things are taboo. The child likes to mess about with everything he can get his hands on, is not yet offended by what comes out of his body, and belches with pleasure when he has eaten a good meal.

Soon he will have to learn to be clean, to distinguish between what is 'done' and 'not done',
but the civilised adult, though pressed into conformity, will always have within him a nostalgia for the time when he thought himself free to do as he liked.

'A being that can adapt to anything: that, in my view, is the best possible definition of man'.

Luce Janin-Devillars,
psychologist

The drinkers, by the Flemish painter Adrien Brouwer (17th century). Musée des Beaux-Arts, Caen.

READING THE LABEL

The label on a bottle of beer gives information as to its origin and character. Labels vary from country to country, with, as yet, no general agreement on what information should be required by law. In Belgium, for instance, there is no legal obligation to state where a beer was brewed, and some beers, brewed 'to order' by this or that manufacturer, bear only the brand name. In countries such as France and Germany, the brewery of origin must be stated, even though it is sometimes presented in the form of a postal code.

It is becoming increasingly common to indicate the

The history of beer, as illustrated by the Liebig company at the turn of the century

alcoholic strength of a beer in terms of the percentage of alcohol in a given volume – written '% vol.' – thus bringing beer into line with other alcoholic drinks. But other systems are still in use: in North America, a beer's strength is indicated in terms of alcohol by weight, giving a lower figure than the by-volume measurement.

It is also common to indicate a beer's density. In Britain, this is still often expressed on a scale beginning at 1000: a very light beer might register 1030, a stout or barley wine 1100. Density may also be indicated in degrees Plato, on a scale ranging from 7 to 30.

To sum up, a typical European pilsner (of German or Alsatian origin) would rate between 4.6 and 5.6 percent by volume or 3.7 and 4.3 percent by weight; while its density would be between 1044 and 1050, or 11 and 12 degrees on the Plato scale. Finally, in Europe at least, it is virtually obligatory to state a 'best before' date.

There follows a glossary of terms used for different national and local specialities:

ABBAYE: a Belgian top-fermentation beer, relatively strong and dense, often subject to a secondary fermentation in the bottle. In colour, an abbey beer may be blond, amber or brown.

ALCOHOL FREE: the term used for any beer containing less than 1 percent alcohol by volume. Beers of this type may be blond, amber or brown in colour.

ALE: a British top-fermentation beer, of only average alcoholic strength, which may be amber-coloured, light or dark. The different varieties are pale ale; mild, which is sweeter, and lower in both alcohol and hops; bitter; stout; and barley wine (see below for further details).

ALT: the German term for top-fermentation beers. Alt means 'old', as contrasted with the more recent bottom-fermentation pilsners. The Düsseldorf breweries specialise in beers of this kind.

BARLEY WINE: term used for the strongest, densest British ales.

BITTER: the most popular type of British ale, drunk mainly in pubs. It has a distinctly hoppy flavour. Colours range from amber to orangey.

BLANCHE: a Belgian wheat beer, often flavoured with spices. As it is not filtered, a 'white' beer can be distinguished by its cloudy appearance. It also has a rather acid taste.

BOCK: the German term for a strong beer. A Doppel Bock is even stronger, and brand names often end in -ator. To confuse the issue, in France the term 'bock' is used to describe a very light beer (under 3.5 percent ABV) and the small 12.5 centilitre glass used in cafés.

BIERE DE GARDE: this term indicates that the beer has been kept longer than is normally the case. It is also used to describe a style of beer specific to French-speaking Flanders.

GUEUZE: a Belgian beer obtained by blending old and young lambic beers (see below). It is refermented in champagne-type bottles.

HELL: the German term for the most commonly drunk type of pilsner. It refers to their pale colour, as compared with the darker Munich beers.

KRIEK: a lambic in which cherries have been steeped for several months. The success of these fruit beers has led to experiments with raspberries (frambozen), blackcurrants, plums, and even bananas.

LAGER: a German word, whose primary meaning is 'to store', with reference to the practice of keeping bottom-fermentation beers in cool conditions. Nowadays, it describes any ordinary bottom-fermentation beer. Though most are blond in colour, Germany has some dark varieties.

LAMBIC: A Belgian beer made with barley, wheat and hops, which is left to ferment spontaneously, then aged for between one and two years. A speciality of the Brussels area, lambic is served in its natural state only in a few Belgian bars. It is blended to give gueuze, and sugar is added to obtain faro.

LIE: the yeasty sediment found in beers which undergo a secondary fermentation in the bottle. Many of these come from Belgium.

LUXE: an official term used in France to indicate beers with an ABV rating of between 4 and 5 percent. It has nothing to do with quality.

PILS: this term derives from the Czech town of Plzen (German: Pilsen), where the first bottom-fermentation blond beers were brewed. Virtually synonymous with the word lager, it is nowadays generally used to describe any blond beer of this type. In Germany, the term Pilsener, or Pilsner, is more likely to describe a well-hopped beer.

PORTER: a British top-fermentation beer (associated mainly with London), dark in colour

and well hopped. It has been dying out, but fortunately some of the micro-breweries have come to its defence.

PREMIUM: in the United States, this term is used to describe a quality lager, denser and more golden in colour than the average. The term is used commercially and in advertising to suggest something stronger than run-of-the-mill beers.

PURE MALT: in France particularly, this term describes beers brewed solely from malted barley. No maize, rice or maltose syrup is added, as happens with most bottom-fermentation beers.

RAUCHBIER: German beer with a smoky flavour, obtained by drying the malt over beech chippings. A speciality of the Bamberg region.

SPECIAL: official term used in France to describe beers with an ABV rating in excess of 5 percent, whatever the style. In Belgium, the term describes all beers other than pilsners and gueuzes.

STOUT: a British top-fermentation beer, brewed with heavily roasted malts to give a completely black colour. The Irish style is dense and dry in taste, though not particularly strong, while the British version is sweeter and more rounded.

TRAPPISTE: Belgian top-fermentation beer brewed by the monks of Trappist monasteries. There are five of them in Belgium, and one in the Netherlands.

WEISSE-WEIZENBIER: German beer brewed from wheat and barley, a speciality of Berlin, Bremen, Bavaria and the Baden region. It differs somewhat from Belgian white beers, being more golden in colour and in some cases quite dark. A thirst-quenching beer, it is drunk mainly in summer.

BIERE DE LA PATRIE

225

SOME BASIC RULES OF BEER DRINKING

When you know something about beer, where it comes from and how it is brewed, tasting becomes a source of real interest and pleasure. There are nevertheless a few simple but vital rules to be borne in mind. Never forget that beer is a fragile biological product, extremely sensitive to temperature and light. If it is kept or served in inappropriate conditions, it may be spoiled and its best qualities destroyed. It would be a shame if, through ignorance, the work of several months – and the brewer's lifetime skill and experience – were set at nought.

Keeping beer Whether it is to be drunk at home or away, beer needs to be kept cool, away from light and sources of heat. However, excessively low temperatures – below 5°C – are equally harmful. The bottle can be kept in any position, except in the case of beers with a sediment or those with a cork stopper, which must be kept upright. If dense beers have been transported, it is wise to let them rest for a few days before drinking.

As a general rule, the younger a beer is drunk the better. There is no point in building up stocks: a

beer begins to deteriorate within six months of purchase. The exceptions to this rule are dense beers (stouts, old ales, certain *bières de garde*), which mature in the bottle. A good example is the British Thomas Hardy ale, which goes on improving for five years after bottling. But these are rare exceptions, and the brewer is always careful to make it known on the label.

Temperature This is a matter of vital importance, all too often overlooked. The basic principle is simple: the stronger and denser a beer, the higher the serving temperature, on a scale ranging from 6-7°C to 16°C. For example, a pilsner or lager with an ABV rating of 5 percent should be served at 7°C, while a top-fermentation amber beer would be just right at between 10 and 12°C.

The exception that proves the rule are British ales: although relatively low in alcohol, they need to be drunk at temperatures in excess of 10°C – always provided they are served on draught, i.e. in a pub. Though a lukewarm beer is undoubtedly unpleasant to drink, never add ice cubes: they cause an immediate release of carbon dioxide and so 'kill' all taste. Serving a beer excessively cold is just as bad: at below 6°C even a light or alcohol-free beer loses its taste and becomes indigestible. Unfortunately, this bad habit is gaining ground as refrigerators become the norm.

The glass There are hundreds, if not thousands, of different shapes of glass – no less than there are beers – and the major brewers make a point of finding the form best suited to their products. Beware of glasses with a bell-shaped rim and of goblets: as with champagne, the head and the aroma of the beer will tend to dissipate too quickly.

Whatever the shape of the glass, the important thing is to keep it clean. A beer glass must be completely free of grease, as any trace of fat causes a rapid release of CO_2 and a consequent deterioration of the beer. Simply wash the glass with a minimum of washing-up liquid, rinse it thoroughly and let it dry by itself: drying-up cloths always harbour traces of grease and detergent, so avoid using them. Before pouring a beer, moisten the glass slightly: if it is too dry, again it will cause too rapid a release of the dissolved gases.

This advice also applies to stoneware beer mugs and other containers not made of conventional glass.

The head Apart from British ales and certain specialities which, because of the way they are made, have a low CO_2 content, most beers nowadays are served with a generous collar of froth, at least $1/2$ inch thick. Not only does it look good, it also ensures that the beer retains its qualities for as long as possible in the glass. The head effectively insulates the beer from the destructive effects of the oxygen in the atmosphere.

This also explains why a bottle of beer should be poured in one go, provided of course that the glass is big enough. The only exceptions to this are beers with a sediment. These should be poured slowly and gently, to ensure that the sediment does not contaminate the beer. It has played its part in conditioning the product; there is no need to drink it!

BEER TASTING

Like a good wine or brandy, a beer should be examined, consulted, sniffed at and savoured before it is consigned to the stomach. Its colour and brilliance, aroma and fragrance are just as important as its impact on the palate.

As this book attests, the world has thousands of beers to offer, belonging to several well-defined and quite distinct families. The more one comes to recognise a beer's characteristics, the greater the pleasure in drinking it.

Colour is, of course, the first thing one notices, though it is not on its own sufficient to define the style of a beer. From palest pale to blackest black, there is an infinite range of subtlety.

Of the many gradations of blond, the most attractive are undoubtedly the honey-coloured beers of exceptional brightness and clarity. But those with a coppery hue, tending to red, are also a delight to the eye.

The large family of amber beers probably comes in more shades than any other: pale brown, tawny, rosé, reddish brown, ochre – the range is extensive and colours often difficult to define. Then there are the brown beers, which may be very dark indeed, though only the velvety British and Irish stouts are of a perfect opaque black, totally impervious to light.

Clarity and brightness, particularly in the case of a blond beer, are signs that it has been expertly brewed and kept. But cloudiness is not necessarily a defect: in the case of unfiltered wheat beers, such as the Belgian whites, the brewer intended that it should be so.

It is pleasant to hear the discreet sound of bubbles bursting in the glass, but more useful to test its nose. The beer may have a fragrance of malt or of yeast, or again a hint of herbs. However, the aroma should never be excessive.

The physical sensation of taking a beer into the mouth is the most revealing of all: one brew takes the taste buds by storm, satisfying the palate with its strength and density; another feels flat and lacking in body. Some really rich beers need to be chewed rather than drunk!

Bitterness is the single most important characteristic of a beer, and an excellent criterion of definition, since it may range from an almost total absence to an extreme of hoppiness. The human palate recognises four main types of taste: sweet, salt, sour and bitter. The latter is the least appreciated of all, though it plays a vital role in quenching thirst.

Maltiness, too, is of vital concern, since it makes all the difference between a flavoursome beer and one that is insipid. Malt gives body, but also mildness

own: the acidity of wheat beers, the caramel taste of brown ales, or the cherry flavour of Belgian krieks.

and a rounded feel, in contrast with the bitterness of hops. This dialogue is further enriched by a third group of flavours, which may be summarised by the term fruitiness. Specialist beer tasters (at the National Taste Laboratory) claim to have detected in beer the flavours of coffee, cereals, toast, liquorice, lemon, tea, violets, and many more.

Some beers have special characteristics of their

A BEER FOR ALL HOURS OF THE DAY

Some beers are best drunk at a certain time of day. For instance, a well-hopped pilsner is excellent as an aperitif, it being proven that hops tend to stimulate the appetite. White beers serve a similar purpose, or may be drunk as a thirst-quencher at any time when the weather is hot.

Denser beers with a richer flavour are to be recommended later in the day, aiding relaxation before the pleasures of the table.

Where really strong beers are concerned – a Munich Doppel Bock or Belgian triple – they are best drunk after the evening meal, to be sipped in the same manner as a really good brandy.

HOW AND WHEN TO SERVE DIFFERENT STYLES OF BEER

STYLE	ORIGIN	CHARACTERISTICS	SERVING	GOES WITH
Pilsner	France, Belgium Germany	bottom fermentation	8°C	Aperitif, light sauces, sorbets
Brown beers	France, Belgium	Well roasted malts	12-14°C	Meats and game with sauces
White beers	Belgium, Germany	Top fermentation, barley and wheat	8°C	Aperitif, sauces for white fish
Abbey beers	Belgium	Top fermentation	10-12°C	Meats prepared with sauces, cheese
Bières de garde	Flanders	Top fermentation	10°C	Meats prepared with sauces, digestive
Gueuzes	Belgium	Spontaneous fermentation	10-12°C	Aperitif, grills, sorbets
Ales	Britain	Top fermentation	10°C	Aperitif, red meat
Stouts	Ireland, Britain	Top fermentation	12-14°C	Afternoon, excellent with oysters

BEER AS AN INGREDIENT AND AS AN ACCOMPANIMENT TO FOOD

Beer has long been used as an ingredient in Belgian cookery, though not very extensively. *Carbonade flamande* – pieces of beef cooked with beer and onions – is the dish you are most likely to encounter, and as a rule beer is used mainly in meat or poultry stews (e.g. coq à la bière), dense beers being a good alternative to wine. When cooked, the residual sugars they contain add a hint of caramel to the flavour of the meat.

A traditional British snack is welsh rarebit. Cheshire or cheddar cheese is melted in beer, with mustard, then spread on slices of bread, toasted under the grill and served hot – with a good ale, of course.

Finally, in certain fish recipes, beer can be used instead of wine in the *court-bouillon* sauce. This is especially appropriate for freshwater fish such as carp. Similarly, in Belgium, mussels are often cooked with beer (preferably a gueuze): *moules marinières à la bière*.

Long neglected by top chefs, beer is now beginning to claim their attention, especially in Alsace. This new interest is evident in *Toqués de Bière*, a book which brings together the recipes of nine chefs from the region, several of them with Michelin stars to their name.

The main challenge with all beer cookery is to retain the bitter and malty aromas specific to the beer, as they are highly volatile and can easily be lost during cooking. But there is an opposite danger of obtaining too concentrated a flavour, which could mask the other ingredients.

Chefs who have investigated this phenomenon often leave the beer to simmer very slowly for long periods. In this way, they may obtain less than a half-litre of sauce from 5 litres of beer, adding it to

ENTRÉES

Potjevlesch
(pâté made with beer and juniper berries)
by Ghislaine Arabian (Ledoyen, Paris)

Ingredients:
1 young rabbit
1 chicken
500g /1lb pie veal
500g/1lb loin of pork
4ltr/7 pints lager beer
thyme
bay leaf
30 juniper berries
15 cloves garlic
salt and pepper
5 leaves gelatine

Method: bone the rabbit and chicken (or get your supplier to do it for you); cut all the other meat into cubes.
Marinade the pieces in the beer for 24 hrs, together with the thyme, bay leaf, juniper berries, garlic, salt and pepper.
Take a large terrine with a lid and build up layers as follows: the four meats; 2 leaves of gelatine; the four meats, 2 leaves of gelatine; the four meats, one leaf of gelatine. Then add the liquid from the marinade.
Cover the terrine.
Cook for 3 hrs in a preheated oven at 180°C/350°F/Gas Mark 4 in a bain-marie, then leave for a further 2 hrs after switching off the oven.
Wait 48 hrs before opening the terrine. Serve cold in slices.

the dish in the final stage of cooking. The beery flavours then counterbalance the other aromas, enhancing the dish as a whole. Beer can also be used to advantage in jellied dishes, particularly jellied trout and jellied eels.

Finally, ice-creams, sorbets and granitas made with fruit-flavoured or abbey beers are most refreshing and make an interesting change.

What beer to drink with a given dish is largely unexplored territory. Most wine waiters have received little training in this field and are poorly placed to advise their customers. Here, then, is fertile ground for experimentation: white fish can be served with a well-hopped beer; rich meats with a *bière de garde*; pork delicacies with a Munich beer; while fruit-flavoured beers are a suitable accompaniment to desserts.

To return to the monastic tradition (the monks often produced cheese as well as beer), there are many cheeses that are better enjoyed with beer than with wine. Some good examples are munster and livarot, both soft cheeses, or harder types such as reblochon, saint-nectaire, tommes of various kinds, cheddar and mimolette.

Being made from the same raw material (a cereal of some kind), beer and bread naturally go well together, especially in the case of rye, wholemeal and multi-grain loaves.

Whether straightforward or more complex examples of the chef's art, the recipes that follow illustrate the wide range of dishes in which beer has a part to play.

Petits légumes à la bière

(Vegetables cooked in beer)

Ingredients for 8 servings:
1 small cauliflower
4 courgettes (zucchini)
3 tomatoes
1 cucumber
2 onions
50g/2oz butter
250ml/9 fl oz lager beer
350ml/12 fl oz cream
salt and pepper

Method: break up the cauliflower into individual florets. Peel the courgettes (zucchini) and cut into cubes. Blanch both vegetables for 3 mins in boiling salted water.

Skin the tomatoes and cucumber and remove the pips, then cut them into cubes. Chop the onions.

Take a large frying pan and sauté the onions in the butter, without letting them go brown. Cook the diced tomatoes for 5 mins, stirring from time to time. Then add the other vegetables, salt and pepper to taste, and the beer.

Cook over a medium heat for roughly 15 mins, until most of the liquid has boiled away.

Transfer the vegetables to individual ramekins and top with the fresh cream. Add salt and pepper if necessary. Brown for 10 minutes in a hot oven at 200°C/400°F/Gas Mark 6.

Welsh rarebit

Ingredients for 4 servings:
250g/¹/2lb Cheshire or Cheddar cheese
200ml/7 fl oz pale ale
1 soup-spoon mild English mustard
pepper
4 slices of bread

Method: cut the cheese into thin slices, put them in a saucepan, add the beer, mustard and a pinch of pepper. Heat the mixture and keep stirring until runny and thoroughly mixed.

Grill the bread and spread with butter. Put each slice on an individual buttered heat-proof plate; spread with the cheese mixture; put the plates under the grill or into a hot oven for 3 to 4 mins; then serve hot.

As a traditional mid-morning or afternoon snack, Welsh rarebit should be accompanied by a good ale. It can also be served as a hot starter.

Terrine de porc et maquereaux

(Pork and mackerel pâté)

by Patrick Cirotte (Le Grenadin, Paris)

Ingredients for 8 servings:
1 half-head of pork
3 carrots
3 onions
3 shallots
1 garlic bulb
3 mackerel
300ml/11 fl oz beer
salt and pepper

Method: cook the half-head of pork for 3 hrs in stock with the vegetables and cloves of garlic. Once cold, remove the brawn, keeping the tongue and brain apart.

Fillet the mackerel and dry-fry the fillets in a non-stick pan.

Heat the juices from the head of pork until half the liquid has simmered away. Add the beer at the last moment. Allow to cool.

Take a terrine and arrange the brawn and mackerel fillets in layers – covered with the beer jelly – until the terrine is full.

Cook in a bain-marie in a hot oven (200°C/400°F/Gas Mark 6) for 30 mins, then leave the terrine to cool in the refrigerator for at least 12 hrs.

Turn out the pâté, cut into slices and serve with a salad (chicory recommended).

Soupe paysanne à la bière

(Farmhouse soup made with beer)

by Marc Wucher (Le Parc, Obernai)

Ingredients for 6 servings:
200g/7oz streaky bacon
200g/7oz savoy cabbage
200g/7oz white cabbage
100g/4oz turnips
200g/7oz celery
100g/4oz leeks
100g/4oz cultivated mushrooms
50g/2tbsps butter
750ml/1¼ pints lager beer
1.5ltr/3 pints stock
300g/11oz grated potatoes
half a French stick
80g/3oz grated gruyère cheese
pinch paprika
chervil

Method: cut the bacon into chunks. Peel and cut up the vegetables into strips. Sauté the bacon in the butter until brown, add the vegetables, and leave to steam for a few minutes in a covered saucepan.

Soak with the beer and boil well before adding the stock and grated potatoes. Leave to simmer for 1 hr.

Make cheese croûtes by cutting the French stick into slices, sprinkling with grated gruyère and paprika and toasting gently in the oven. Serve the hot soup on the croûtes, adding a sprinkling of chopped chervil.

Coquilles Saint-Jacques aux endives et à la bière

(Scallops prepared with chicory and beer)

by Yvan (Restaurant Yvan, Paris)

Ingredients for 4 servings:
4 head chicory
salt and pepper
pinch sugar
nutmeg
12 scallops
100ml/4 fl oz fish stock
100ml/4 fl oz lager beer

Method: sauté the chicory in a pan with a knob of butter, seasoning them with salt, pepper, sugar and a sprinkling of nutmeg. Keep them warm.

Now fry the scallops for 3 mins, seasoning with salt and pepper. Mix the fish stock and beer, thicken with butter and add further seasoning if necessary. Arrange each plate with the chicory in the centre, surrounded by scallops; top with the sauce and serve immediately.

FISH DISHES

Merlans frits à la bière

(Whiting fried in beer)

Ingredients for 6 servings:
6 whiting
100g/¹/4lb flour
cooking oil
4 shallots
30g/2tbsps butter
250ml/¹/2 pint brown beer
chervil

Method: Gut and wash the whiting, season with salt and dip in flour. Fry until golden, then leave to drain on absorbent paper.
Pre-heat the oven to (200°C/400°F/Gas Mark 6). Chop the shallots and fry them gently in the butter. Add the beer and simmer for 10 mins, until the liquid is reduced by half. Season with salt and pepper and add the chopped chervil.
Place the whiting on a large buttered dish and cover with the beer sauce. Pop them in the oven for 10-15 mins and serve hot.

Sandre en meunière et sabayon

(Perch meunière with sabayon!)
by Gilles Epié (Le Miraville, Paris)

Ingredients for 4 servings:
400g/³/4lb celeriac
400ml/14 fl oz groundnut oil
600g/1¹/4lbs perch fillets
200g/¹/2lb butter
salt and pepper
500ml/1 pint Gold de Kanterbräu beer
200g/¹/2lb butter
2 egg yolks
chives
dill

Method: peel the celeriac and grate very finely. Heat the oil and fry the celeriac until crisp and golden, drain and keep warm.
Divide the perch fillets into four portions. Gently melt the butter in a saucepan then clarify.
Fry the perch fillets in a pan with a small amount of butter and oil until golden (3 mins for one side, 2 mins for the other), seasoning with salt and pepper. Keep warm.
Heat the beer in a saucepan. Beat the egg yolks and continue to do so as you add the beer. Simmer over a low heat, beating all the time, until the sabayon begins to thicken. Blend in the clarified butter.
Lay the perch fillets on warm plates, sprinkle with chives and chopped dill, and arrange the fried celeriac round the outside.
Serve the sabayon separately in a sauce boat.

MEAT AND POULTRY DISHES

Carbonade à la flamande

Ingredients for 4 servings:
750g/1¹/2lbs beef (flank or chuck)
40g/3tbsps lard
250g/¹/2lb onions
1 bunch mixed herbs
750ml/1¹/2 pints amber or brown beer
1 glass beef stock
25g/2tbsps butter
25g/2tbsps flour
¹/2tsp brown sugar
salt and pepper

Method: cut up the beef and brown it in a hot frying pan with the lard. Remove and drain the pieces. Cut the onions into thin slivers and sauté in the same fat. Now arrange the meat and onions in alternate layers in a casserole dish, season and add the mixed herbs.
Reheat the frying pan, adding the beer and the beef stock. In another pan, melt the butter and stir in the flour, then blend in the beer mixture and add the brown sugar. Season and pour this liquid into the casserole. Cover and simmer as gently as possible for 2 ¹/2 hrs. Serve straight from the casserole.

Foie de veau rôti aux oignons et aux cerises

(Roast calf's liver with onions and cherries)

by Bernard Broux (Le Graindorge, Paris)

Ingredients for 4 servings:
4 large onions
50g/2tbsps butter
50g/2oz sugar
1 small jar of cherries preserved in vinegar
500ml/³/4 pint beer
1 thick cut of calf's liver weighing 700-800g/1¹/2-1³/4lbs

Method: place the onions – unskinned – on an oven-proof dish and bake gently at 180°C/350°F/Gas Mark 4, for 2 hrs.
Next peel the onions and cut them into large rings. Melt the butter in a frying pan, then add the onions, the sugar and the vinegar from the cherries. Cook for 30 mins, then add the beer.
Allow the liquid to simmer away until the sauce has a glazed look to it.
Meanwhile, season the slab of calf's liver and roast in a preheated oven at 190°C/375°F/Gas Mark 5, for 15-20 mins but ensure that the centre remains pink (60°C/140°F on a meat thermometer).
Add the cherries to the onion sauce, arrange them on the bottom of the dish, slice the liver add to the sauce and serve hot.

Pintade rôtie à la bière et au gingembre

(Roast guinea fowl with beer and ginger)

by Michel Rostang (Paris)

Ingredients for 4 servings:
1 guinea fowl weighing 1.5 kg/3¹/2lbs, (gutted, cleaned and prepared)
550ml/1 pint beer
1 inch ginger root
100ml/4 fl oz rice vinegar
60g/2oz carrots
60g/2oz onions
3 cloves garlic
50ml/2 fl oz groundnut oil
thyme
bay leaf
50g/3tbsps butter
150ml/5 fl oz chicken stock
Accompaniments
4 potatoes
8 thin rashers smoked bacon
salt and pepper

Method: put the guinea fowl in a deep dish and marinade with the beer for at least 8 hrs (turning it at the half-way stage).
Peel and finely grate the ginger, and soak it in the rice vinegar for 1 hr.
Peel and dice the carrots, onions and garlic.
Drain the guinea fowl, season with salt and pepper, and fry in hot oil in a casserole dish until golden. Turn and baste it at regular intervals for 10 mins.

To make the accompaniment: peel the potatoes, cut them into slices 1cm/¹/2inch thick, then into rectangles 6x3cm/2¹/2 x 1¹/2inches. Arrange them on an oven-proof dish and surround with rashers of bacon. Grease the potatoes with the fat from the guinea fowl and roast for 20 mins in a preheated oven at 200°C/400°F/Gas Mark 6, basting frequently.

When the guinea fowl has finished cooking, drain and keep warm. Remove the fat from the casserole and add the vegetables, thyme, bay leaf and chopped carcase. Brown for 5 mins with 30g/2tbsps of butter, add the marinade and vinegar and boil away a quarter of the liquid. Add the chicken stock and boil away another quarter of the liquid. Strain off the solids, add the grated ginger, 100ml/4 fl oz of beer and 20g/1tbsp of butter and reduce the resulting liquid down to half its volume.

Cut up the white meat and thighs of the guinea fowl, arrange on plates and top with the sauce. Serve with the potato and bacon accompaniment.

Lapereau aux pruneaux

(Rabbit with prunes)

Ghislaine Arabian (Ledoyen, Paris)

Ingredients for 4 servings:
1 young rabbit
3ltr/5 1/2 pints beer for the marinade

For making the sauce:
the green part of a leek
1 carrot
1 onion
1 clove garlic
1 stick celery
1 sprig thyme
1 bay leaf
200g/7oz prunes
1 tsp strong mustard
30g/2tbsps brown sugar
1 small bar plain chocolate

Method: bone and joint the rabbit, but keep the thighs and saddle joints whole. Put the meat in a cool place. Marinade the carcase and bones in beer for 24 hrs.

Next prepare the vegetables for the sauce, cutting them into small pieces. Remove the carcase and bones from the beer, dry them and brown them in a hot oven.

Return them to the beer, together with the vegetables, add 1ltr/1 3/4 pints of water and bring to the boil. Cover and leave to cook for 4 or 5 hrs. Then strain the liquid through a sieve and reduce it by three quarters to obtain a sauce.

Soak the prunes for 1 hr in lukewarm water. Dab the rabbit on the inside of the thighs and saddle joints with the mustard, stuff them with prunes and tie up with string.

Pre-heat the oven to 190°C/375°F/Gas Mark 5. Quickly brown the rabbit joints in a slightly greased frying pan, then cook them in the oven (20 mins for the thighs; 10 mins for the saddle joints).

Complete the sauce by blending in the brown sugar, the chocolate and a few prunes. Leave it to cook for 10 mins.

Top the rabbit joints with the sauce and serve with boiled potatoes or fresh pasta.

Roulades de porc

(Pork roulades)

Ingredients for 6 servings:
6 shallots
parsley
4 fennel bulbs
100g/4oz butter
6 small escalopes of pork
250g/1/2lb small onions
750g/1 1/2lbs potatoes
250ml/1/2 pint beer
250ml/1/2 pint stock
salt and pepper
250ml/1/2 pint double cream

Method: use a blender to purée the shallots, parsley and one chopped fennel bulb. Simmer this purée with a little of the butter for 15 mins.

Lay the escalopes on a board, season them with salt and pepper and spread thinly with a little of the purée. Roll up the slices of meat and tie with string. Peel the onions and potatoes and cut the remaining fennel bulbs into quarters.

Sauté the potatoes and whole onions in the butter. When they are a nice golden colour, remove them from the pan, keep warm, and replace them with the roulades, which need to be well browned all over. Then put back the onions, potatoes and fennel. Pour the beer and stock over the contents of the pan, and add seasoning if necessary.

Cook for 25 mins in an uncovered frying pan. Arrange the roulades and vegetables on a serving dish. Add cream to the remaining juices and bring to the boil. Use as a sauce for the meat and vegetables.

DESERTS

Munster à la bière
by Fernand Mischler,
(Le Cheval Blanc, Lembach)

Ingredients for 4 servings:
1 ripe munster cheese
2 tbsp Dijon mustard
100ml/4 fl oz lager beer
cumin
walnut bread

Method: blend the mustard with the beer and whip for 2 to 3 mins to obtain a frothy sauce. Place the munster on a plate, top with the sauce and add some cumin. Serve with walnut bread.

Tarte à la bière

Ingredients for 6 servings:
shortcrust pastry
200g/7oz caster sugar
2 eggs
200ml/7 fl oz lager beer
35g/2tbsps butter

Method: roll out the pastry and use it to line a shallow baking tin. Spread the sugar evenly over the pastry.
Beat the eggs, add the beer, and pour the mixture gently over the sugar. Add some small knobs of butter and bake in the oven (220°C/425°F/Gas Mark 7) for 35 mins.

Pommes au four et sorbet à la bière
(Baked apples and beer sorbet)
by José Martinez (15 Montaigne, Paris)

Ingredients for 4 servings:
for the sorbet:
250g/8oz sugar
1ltr/1¹/2 pints water
500ml/³/4 pint Gold de Kanterbräu beer
5g/1tsp glucose
120ml/4oz sugar syrup

20g/1oz pistachio nuts
20g/1oz caster sugar
40g/2tbsps butter
4 top-quality apples

Method: for the sorbet, heat the sugar and water in a saucepan until it caramelises. Add this to the beer, together with the glucose and sugar syrup, mix well and transfer to an ice-cream maker.
Finely chop the pistachios and beat with the sugar and butter to make a cream.
Wash and dry the apples, and hollow them out on the side opposite to the stalk, without boring right through. Fill with the pistachio butter and bake for 1¹/2 hrs (180°C/350°F/Gas mark 4).
Serve the apples hot, with two scoops of the sorbet.

Mousse moka-bière

by Olivier Simon (L'Entre-Siècle, Paris)

Ingredients for ten servings:

for the coffee syrup:
5 large cups of strong coffee (mocha)
50ml/4tbsps liquid coffee extract
300ml/$^1/_2$ pint brown beer

3 egg yolks
3 leaves gelatine
6 egg whites
100ml/4 fl oz sugar syrup*
2 tbsp icing sugar
500ml/$^3/_4$ pint single cream

Method: heat the ingredients for the coffee syrup until a light syrup is obtained.

Beat the 3 egg yolks and add the syrup, which should still be boiling hot. Add the gelatine leaves, having first softened them in cold water and dried them. Keep beating until the mixture has cooled.

Whisk the egg whites in an electric blender until stiff and add the hot sugar syrup in fine dribbles. Continue blending and incorporate the icing sugar. Allow to cool.

Whip the fresh cream until stiff and, without letting it flop, fold in the coffee extract and the egg whites. Refrigerate for 2 hrs.

On each plate, arrange three blobs of the mousse interspersed with thin biscuits – see illustration. Serve chilled but not frozen.

* Use the following proportions to make the syrup: 1kg/2lbs sugar to every 750ml/1$^1/_4$ pints water. Heat to 120°C/248°F.

Gelée de pamplemousse

(Grapefruit jelly)

by Pierre Gagnaire (Saint-Étienne)

Ingredients for 10 servings:

1kg/2$^1/_4$lbs pink-fleshed grapefruit
100g/4oz sugar, plus the weight in sugar of the grapefruit rinds
1ltr/1$^3/_4$ pints lager beer
10 leaves gelatine

For the pear juice:
5 ripe pears
30g/1oz sugar
juice of 3 lemons

For the nut topping:
80g/2$^1/_2$oz sugar
100g/4oz walnuts

Method: peel the grapefruits with a knife and cut them into large cubes. Separate the flesh from the skins of the segments. Retain the juice. Mix the flesh with 100g/4oz of sugar and keep in a cool place.

Blanch the rinds for 5 mins in boiling water. Repeat 3 times, cooling and drying the rinds each time. Simmer them in a saucepan for 1 $^1/_2$ hrs together with their own weight in sugar.

Boil a quarter of the beer with the grapefruit juice, soften and add the gelatine. Beat the juice and add it to the flesh and preserved rinds of the grapefruit. Leave overnight in a cool place, then add the remaining beer.

For the pear juice, peel, cut up and remove the cores from the pears, then blend them in a mixer with the sugar and lemon juice. Strain and keep in a cool place.

For the nut topping, take a thick-bottomed casserole and make a caramel with the sugar and a little water in a heavy-based saucepan. Add the walnuts and stir well to ensure they are completely coated in the mixture. Turn out onto a greased baking tray and allow to cool.

Arrange each plate with the jelly in the middle, surrounded by the pear juice, and with a sprinkling of caramelised walnuts.

Sorbet à la bière

by Jean-Marie Meulien (Paris)

Ingredients:

1ltr/1³/4 pints water
20g/1oz sugar
20ml/1tbsp white vinegar
250ml/¹/2 pint beer (blond or pale amber)

Method: make a syrup with the sugar and water, then add the vinegar. Transfer to an ice cream maker. As soon as the mixture begins to set, add a quarter of the beer.
Once the sorbet has set, place a scoopful in a tall stemmed glass, add some of the remaining beer, which should be well chilled, and stir to give it a head.

Terrine de fruits en gelée de bière

Ingredients:

10 oranges
250g/8oz strawberries
9 leaves gelatine
500ml/1 pint orange juice
250ml/¹/2 pint lager beer

Method: peel the oranges, divide into segments and remove the skins. Cut up the strawberries. Leave the fruits to drain on absorbent paper.
Soak the gelatine in cold water. Squeeze out any water when soft and melt in a small amount of hot orange juice. Add the remainder of the orange juice and the beer and allow to cool, but not set.
Arrange the orange segments and strawberries in the bottom of a terrine, cover with the liquid, then repeat this operation until the terrine is full.
Place in the refrigerator. When cold, cut the jelly into slices. Try serving with a strawberry sauce.

SIDE DISHES

Navets braisés à la bière

(Turnips braised with beer)

Ingredients for 6 servings:
1kg/2^{1}/4lbs young turnips
30g/2tbsps butter
salt and pepper
500ml/1 pint amber beer
bunch mixed herbs
250ml/^{1}/2 pint stock

Method: peel the turnips and blanch them for 5 mins in boiling salted water. Drain. Brown gently with butter in a large frying pan. Add seasoning. Heat the beer over a medium heat in a large saucepan, then add the mixed herbs, stock and turnips. Bring to the boil, cover and leave to simmer for 15 to 20 mins. The turnips should be tender but remain whole.
Serve hot with a fried meat.

Beurre de houblon

(Hop butter)

by Mme Michel Haag (Brasserie Météor)

Ingredients:
30g/1oz hop cones
30g/1oz lettuce leaves
chopped parsley
250g/8oz butter
salt and pepper

Method: chop up all the ingredients very small and mix well with the butter. Add seasoning to taste. This butter is delicious with toasted farmhouse bread, cold pork meats, salads, etc.

Pain à la bière

(Beer bread)

by Jean-Luc Poujauran

Ingredients:
10g/^{1}/2oz beer yeast (from the baker)
2 tbsp rock salt
330ml/^{3}/4 pint lager beer
500g/1lb flour

Method: mix the yeast with a little water, and dissolve the salt with the beer. Sieve the flour and heap it on a plate with a hollow in the middle. Gradually add the beer, then the yeast, kneading all the time until you obtain an evenly mixed dough. Add a little more water if necessary.
Cover the dough with a cloth and leave in a warm place for 1 ^{1}/2 hrs.
Knead the dough to remove accumulated carbon dioxide, then leave for a further hour or two.
Shape the dough and place on an oven-proof dish, or in a cake tin. Bake in a hot oven 200°C/400°F/Gas mark 6 for 25 mins, with a small ramekin of water to prevent the bread from drying out, having first made a few holes in the top of the loaf.
You can, if you wish, add some hazel nuts or raisins.

BEER HUNTING – AND SOME BREWERS

Finding really good beers can often be more difficult than seems reasonable, and finding a wide variety of really good beers can be even more difficult. The problem is that regional styles generally developed because they were the styles that the people of the region enjoyed, and there may therefore be little demand for unusual beers.

Just dropping into a popular local watering hole is unlikely, therefore, to be much of a revelation: all too often, all you will be served is more of the same sort of beer that the region is noted for. You may even encounter hostility from local drinkers if you ask them where you can find something more interesting. As far as they are concerned, their beer is what they like, and there is no reason to drink anything else. This can be awkward if you are (for example) in Cologne, and have no taste for nondescript beers served in very small glasses.

UNITED KINGDOM

Pubs in Britain are totally unpredictable. Of two pubs which look identical from the outside, one may have nothing but bland, pasteurized beer and the other may offer anything up to half a dozen 'real ales' pumped up from barrels with traditional beer engines. If there are too many 'real ales' though, you need to beware: the turnover of some of the less popular brews may not be high enough to ensure that they are kept in peak condition. Fortunately, most local bookshops carry guides to local 'real ale' pubs, serving beers from breweries such as the ones listed below, or you can get the CAMRA (Campaign for Real Ale) *Good Beer Guide*, published annually. Particular specialities are listed in brackets, though most breweries offer a range of beers.

Banks's, Wolverhampton, West Midlands (mild)

Caledonian, Edinburgh, (various)

Eldridge Pope, Dorchester, Dorset (old ale)

Fuller's, London (bitter)

Gale's, Horndean, Hampshire (old ale)

Greene King, Bury St. Edmunds, Suffolk (various)

Highgate, Walsall, West Midlands (mild)

McEwan's, Edinburgh (Scottish ale)

McMullen, Hertford (mild)

Marstons, Burton-upon-Trent, Staffodshire (various)

Orkney Brewery, Sandwick (various)

Samuel Smith, Tadcaster, Yorkshire (various)

Scottish & Newcastle Breweries, Newcastle upon Tyne (brown)

Theakston, Masham, Yorkshire (old ale)

Traquair, Innerleithen (ales)

Young's, London (various)

UNITED STATES AND CANADA

As recently as the early 1980s, the United States was very bad news for beer lovers: weak, gassy beer, served half frozen, was all you could get in most places. Today, there are many more small breweries, micro-breweries and brew pubs, some of which brew execellent and distinctive beers. Look in the Yellow Pages to find addresses, and call them to see where their beers are sold, or refer to the bibliography in this book. By the time you read this, there are likely to be many more good, small breweries than those listed below, which are in any case only a sampling of possibilities. Particular specialities are listed in brackets, though many breweries also offer other beers.

Alaskan Brewing Company, Juneau, Alaska (alt bier)

Ambier Brewing Company, Milwaukee, Wisconsin, (Viennese lager)

Anchor Brewing Company, San Francisco, California (various)

Anderson Valley, Booneville, Calfornia (oatmeal stout)

Baderbrau, Elmhurst, Illinois (pilsner)

Boston Beer Company, Boston, Massachusetts (American ale)

The Brooklyn Brewery, Brooklyn, New York (brown ale)

Celis Brewery, Austin, Texas (Belgian wheat beer)

Dock Street Brewery and Restaurant, Philadelphia, Pennsylvania (barley wine)

Frankenmuth Brewery, Frankenmuth, Michigan (bock)

Gordon Biersch, Palo Alto, Calfornia (Dortmunder export)

Hart Brewing Company, Kalama, Washington (weizen)

Lakefront Brewery, Milwaukee, Wisconsin (lager)

F.X. Matt, Utica, New York (American ale)

Mendocino Brewing Company, Hopland, California (American ale)

New Amsterdam Company, New York, N.Y., (ale and amber beer)

New Haven Brewing, New Haven, Connecticut (brown ale)

North Coast Brewing, Fort Bragg, California (dry stout)

Niagara Falls Brewing, Niagara Falls, Ontario (various)

Pete's Brewing Company, Palo Alto, California (brown ale)

Portland Brewing Company, Portland, Oregon (American ale)

Redhook, North Seattle, Washington (bitter)

Rockies Brewing Company, Boulder, Colorado (porter)

Publican Brewing Company, Sacramento, California

Saratoga Lager, Englewood, New Jersey (Dortmunder export)

Sherlock's Home, Minnetonka. Minnesota (Scottish ale)

Sierra Nevada Brewing Company, Chico, California (various)

Silver Creek Brewery, Guelph, Ontario (American ale)

Sprecher Brewing Company, Milwaukee, Wisconsin (lager)

Stanislaus Brewing Company, Modesto, California (alt bier)

Stoudt's Real Beer, Adamstown, Pennsylvania (Dortmunder export)

Summit Brewing Company, St. Paul, Minnesota (pale ale)

Wellington County, Guelph, Ontario (bitter)

Widmer Brewing Company, Portland, Oregon (alt bier)

Yakima Brewing and Malting, Yakima, Washington (Scottish ale)

MUSEUMS

BELGIUM

- Anderlecht: the Brasserie Cantillon is working museum, where Jean-Pierre Roy, a scion of the original family, brews lambic beers.
- Antwerp: Maison des Brasseurs.
- Bocholt: Beer museum at the Martens brewery, 1, Reppelerweg – Tel: (11) 47 29 80.
- Brussels: Musée de la Maison des Brasseurs, 10, Grand'Place – Tel: (2) 511 49 87.

The Musée bruxellois de la gueuze is housed in the Cantillon brewery, 56, rue Gueude – Tel: (2) 521 49 28.
- Leuven: Musée municipal de la bière (artefacts a documents).
- Poperinghe: Musée national du houblon (devoted to hops, with artefacts and documents).

DENMARK

- Copenhagen: The Carlsberg Foundation museum has a number of rooms devoted to the history of brewing, illustrated with old equipment and documents.

FRANCE

Musée européen de la bière, Stenay – Rue de la Citadelle 55700 Stenay – Tel: 29 80 68 78 – Open every day from 15 March to 1 November, 10 to 12 a.m. and 2 to 6 p.m. Food cooked with beer is available at the *Taverne du Musée.*

Established in 1986 in a malting dating from the 17th century, the Stenay museum traces the history of beer from the time of Nebuchadnezzar to the present day. Brought together by the museum's curator, Philippe Voluer, the artefacts on display constitute one of the finest collections in Europe. The emphasis is on pre-industrial brewing. Although somewhat off the beaten track, this museum merits a special visit.

Musée français de la brasserie – 62, rue Charles-Courtois 54210 Saint-Nicholas-de-Port – Tel.:83 46 95 52 – Open on Saturdays, Sundays and public holidays in June, from 2 to 6 p.m., then every day from 1 July to 30 September (except Mondays), 2 to 6 p.m.

The museum is housed in the former Vézelise brewery, designed by the architect Fernand César and built in 1920 – an ideal setting in which to illustrate the history of industrial brewing. The collection is being added to all the time. This is the first time a major European brewery has been converted into a museum.

Musée de la bière vosgienne – 88270 Ville-sur-Illon – Tel: 29 36 53 18 – Open in June for groups (by special arrangement) and from 1 July to 20 September on Saturdays and Sundays, 2.30 to 6.30 p.m.

Housed in an authentic 19th-century brewery, the museum was born of the enthusiasm of Bernard Saunier and a local association of volunteers. An attractive feature is that the artefacts are displayed in the old historic buildings: brew house, mill, laboratory and cellars.

Brasserie Sébastien Artois – 14, avenue P.-Brossolette BP 9 – 59426 Armentières Cedex – Tel: 20 48 30 30. Group visits by appointment.

This private museum was created by Bertrand Motte, former chairman of Sébastien Artois, and is housed in the Motte-Cordonnier brewery, whose history goes back to 1650. There are fascinating collections of mugs, bottles and glasses, as well as artefacts formerly used for brewing, racking and transporting the beer. The museum should be visited in conjunction with the brewery as it exists today.

GERMANY

Many German breweries and a number of monasteries have special displays illustrating the history of beer and its manufacture.
The following are of particular interest:
- Bamberg (Bavaria): the brewery of the 11th-century

abbeys of Bamberg is a museum of brewing. Within a roughly 36-mile radius of Bamberg there are reputed to be more then 100 breweries – the highest concentration anywhere in the world.

• Bayreuth: the Maisel brewery. Here, the old brewing installations have been maintained in good order, and there is a room where you can sample various beers.

• Cologne: there has been a brewery on the Gaffel site since 1302, though the present owners have only been there since 1908. The museum is part of the working brewery, but concentrates on drinking vessels and advertising material.

• Cologne: the Kölsch museum (devoted to the city's traditional beer), which is housed in the Küppers brewery.

• Dortmund: nine thousand years of brewing history are illustrated at the Kronen brewery.

• Einbeck: there is a small museum attached to the Einbecker brewery, as well as a pub or "brewery tap" serving Einbeck ales in the Market Square and dating from 1552.

• Essen: Museum of Brewing.

• Hagen: an open-air museum, with plenty of machinery on display.

• Höhr-Grenzhausen (Westerwald): the Rastal company, one of the biggest manufacturers of beer glasses, has set up a museum devoted to mugs, pitchers and other forms of container used in times past.

• Munich: the Löwenbräu Museum.

IRELAND

• Dublin: The Guinness Museum has fine collections illustrating the history of brewing and associated trades (malting, hop-growing and processing, cooperage, etc.), together with a perfect replica of the brewery as it was at the turn of the century. There is an excellent slide show and a superb collection of advertising material for Guinness products over the years.

SWITZERLAND

• Rheinfelden: the Feldschlösschen brewery with its mock Tudor architecture is well worth a visit. It also features some educational displays.

• Winterthur: The museum of technology (Musée des techniques) has a substantial section on brewing.

THE UNITED KINGDOM

• Braemore (Hampshire): museum of pre-industrial brewing, housed in an Elizabethan manor house.
Burton-on-Trent: Bass run a brewing museum and cultural centre devoted to beer.

• Stamford (Lincolnshire): All Saints' Brewery. Founded in 1825 and opened exclusively as a museum from the 1970s to 1992, this reopened as an experimental brewery for making Belgian-style fruit beers with lambic yeasts.

• Tadcaster (North Yorkshire): Tadcaster is something of a site of pilgrimage for beer lovers, even if the John Smith's breweries are owned by the giant Courage combine. There is a small but interesting museum attached to the brewery.

THE UNITED STATES

• Ft. Mitchell, Kentucky: the Oldenberg Brewery and Entertainment Complex features the American Museum of Brewing History and Arts – the world's largest museum devoted to the subject.

• Milwaukee (Wisconsin): Miller offer tours of the brewery. There are dioramas of the brewing process.

• Pottsville (Pennsylvania): D.G. Yuengling's is the oldest continuously operating brewery in the United States and there is a small museum and gift shop attached. During Prohibition they survived by producing soft drinks, yeasts and cereal grains.

• St. Louis (Missouri): although the famous Anheuser-Busch plant does not feature a museum, there are some historical displays and you can take tours of the brewery.

INDEX

Bold type denotes that the beer in question is illustrated by a photograph.

244

X

Y

Z

BIBLIOGRAPHY

The Bedside Book of Beer, Barrie Pepper, Ed., Alma Books, St Albans c. 1990.

Beer Drinker's Companion, John Dallas & Charles McMaster, Edinburgh Publishing Co., 1993

CAMRA Dictionary of Beer (CAMRA - Campaign for Real Ale), Brian Glover, Longman, Harlow 1985.

European Beer Almanac, Roger Protz, Lochar c. 1991.

The Good Beer Guide (CAMRA), Alma Books. St. Albans, annually.

The Good Beer Guide to Belgium and Holland, Tim Webb, compiler, Alma Books, St. Albans. c. 1992.

The Great British Beer Book, Roger Protz, Impact Books 2nd edition 1992.

Michael Jackson's Beer Companion, Michael Jackson, Mitchell Beazley, London 1993.

Michael Jackson's Pocket Beer Book, Michael Jackson, Mitchell Beazley, London 3rd edition c. 1991.

New Beer Guide, Brian Glover, David & Charles, Newton Abbot c. 1988.

New World Guide to Beer, Michael Jackson, Bloomsbury, London 1988.

On Tap, WBR Publications, Clemson, N. Carolina (directory of American brewpubs).

MAGAZINES

All About Beer, Durham, North Carolina (national).

Ale Street News, New Jersey (New York area).

American Brewer, Hayward, California.

BarleyCorn, Falls Church, Virginia (regional).

Beer Enthusiast, catalogue of the Association of Brewers, Boulder, Colorado.

Brewing News, Austin, Texas (regional).

The Celebrator, Hayward, California.

The Pint Pot, Seattle, Washington (regional).

What's Brewing, St. Albans, Herts, UK.

World Beer Review, Clemson, South Carolina.

World of Beer, Milan (international).

ACKNOWLEDGEMENTS

We would like to thank all those who have helped us
in producing this book, in particular:
Jean-Claude and Patrick Lemaire, directors of les Artisans de la Bière,
Champigny-sur-Marne, who supplied the many bottles featured
in the illustrations and shared with us their wide knowledge of
beers from around the world;
Michael Jackson, whose works are a mine of information
for those seeking an introduction to the world of beer;
Élisabeth Pierre, communications director of the Brasseurs de France,
who let us make use of the association's picture archives;
The Kronenbourg and Schutzenberger breweries in France
and the Carlsberg brewery in Denmark, for the
illustrative material they contributed;
Jean-Claude Colin and Bernard Rotman, organisers of the Eurobière
show in Strasbourg, for their advice and friendship;
Zivadin Mitrovic, for information on the brewing
industry in the former Yugoslavia;
brewers from all parts of the world, who sent us
samples of their products.